To Jeanne! May you always stay strong. Warm wishes, Victoria M. Yasika

Wounded But Not Broken

9/11 a Decade

By Victoria M. Yasika

PublishAmerica
Baltimore

PublishAmerica has allowed this work to remain exactly as the author intended, verbatim, without editorial input.

Softcover 9781462645237
PUBLISHED BY PUBLISHAMERICA, LLLP
www.publishamerica.com
Baltimore

Printed in the United States of America

Dedication

First and foremost, I dedicate this book to my Father in Heaven, to my Savior Jesus Christ, and to my Comforter the Holy Spirit. It has been through your Word, your people, and your prompting that I looked at these events with Godly eyes.

To my mother who always showed me what it means to have courage and faith through her life experiences. To my father who always knew how to encourage me to see my dreams come true. To my children, DJ and Tolyk for enduring and understanding during a tremendously challenging time which happened to coincide with their teenage years. My sons, you both brought so much joy and relief by being the wonderful and caring people that you are!

Finally, to my soulmate Guy, without you, I would not have gone back to school nor had the belief in my writing to finish this book. You truly do complete me in so many ways. Thank you for your encouragement, your faith in me, and most importantly I want you to know that "Your Love Amazes Me".

Acknowledgements

A special thanks to our Lord Jesus Christ for His grace, wisdom, and such a sweet relationship with us. Additionally we were blessed with West Essex Baptist Church (Now known as the Crossing Church), the Converge Northeast previously known as the Baptist General Conference, Medford Lakes Community Church, the late Larry Burkett and his listeners, Columbus Baptist Church, Jacobstown Baptist Church, Pastor Tim Chicola who had helped us more times than we can name, Pastor DeMarco who rolled up his sleeves and helped repair cars and came up alongside of us when we needed it. To my mother of course, and my father (now deceased), who were always willing to help even when we did not ask and for the compassion and empathy that they each showed us. There are still many others that have not been named but are as appreciated. A special thanks to our sons DJ and Tolyk for your, modesty, unselfishness, understanding, patience, generosity, love, and respect as we struggled through some of your teenage years with all that had happened, we love you! Finally, to my husband Guy, we drew closer not farther, we loved deeper, we shared more openly, we cried in each other's arms. You held me tightly when I thought I couldn't get through another event and I held you when you needed it. You are my best friend, my husband, my love, and my dream come true. I would not change what we have been through but, I don't want to go through it ever again.

Contents

Chapter One: The mighty do fall 9

Chapter Two: In the Wake...........26

Chapter Three: Humbled...........40

Chapter Four: Manna from Heaven—The Blessings...........47

Chapter Five: In the Valley 57

Chapter Six: Delighting in Trials 69

Chapter Seven: Tomorrow May Not Come 80

Chapter Eight: Death is Precious to the Lord 87

Chapter Nine: Waiting on the Lord...........108

Chapter Ten: Put Not Your Trust in Men 121

Chapter Eleven: New Opportunities 134

Chapter Twelve: Vengence is the Lord's: (and the Navy
Seals' too!) 148

Chapter One
The mighty do fall

On Monday night, I felt a strong need to be home. The air was thick and the skies signaled a storm that could impose great damage. By the time I got home the air cleared, my mood had not.

Vicky met me at the door. She asked what was wrong. She thought it was work related. I just said I feel like something bad is going to happen. We talked a bit which usually calms me down, but not this time. After dinner she asked if I would like to watch TV. I requested something light. Bedtime came and so did my dreams. I woke up thinking I had been shot. I could go on about the dream, suffice it to say, I fixed myself up with some cotton, tin foil and duct tape. I guess it is true. Duct tape can be used for just about anything.

All day on Monday a threatening storm lured overhead. On the farm, the animals were all high-spirited from the electricity in the air. Guy came home in a strange mood. I assumed it was a bad day at work and made a mental note to just avoid any issues that might upset him. When I asked him if he were okay, he said, "I have a feeling something really bad is going to happen."

"Like what?"

"I don't know."

"Like a power outage from the storm?"

"No, something really bad." I shrugged. He probably just needed a good night sleep and would feel better in the morning. We had a rather quiet evening of just relaxing and watching some television and then went to bed.

I was startled by the ringing of the phone. It took me a few seconds to realize it was already morning. As I groggily answered the phone, I glanced at the alarm clock. It was 8:50 a.m. I also glanced at the caller I.D. and grunted. It was my father-in-law calling early because he's retired and gets up with the chickens.

"Hello"

"Vicky, it's Dad. Do you have the television on?"

"No. Why?" I said with a little irritability. (I didn't even have the coffee on yet).

"Where's Guy?"

"At work, why Dad? What's wrong?" By this point, I was quite puzzled at the urgency in his voice. So I put on the television not even asking what channel I should turn to. And then my world changed. A plane had just flown into Tower One of the World Trade Center.

"Dad, I'll call Guy and get back to you."

Guy worked in Tower One of the World Trade Center on the 78th floor. I called Guy at work and just got the voice mail. Well it must not be too bad if the voice mail is still working, I thought. I went back to the television with sleepy eyes and tried to figure out what just happened. Was this an accident? Was this real? Was this a movie preview? Nothing computed. Nothing made any sense. At that moment, I watched in disbelief as a plane flew into Tower Two. This wasn't an accident. This wasn't a movie. This was real! But who would do such a thing and why? More questions started to pour through my mind that wouldn't receive any answers. At the same time, phone calls also began pouring in. Time after time, I had to tell the callers that no, I don't know if Guy is all right, and no I haven't heard from him, and yes, I will call them as soon as I know. As I hung up the phone the doorbell rang and my neighbor came in with shock in her eyes. She hugged me and immediately prayed with me. We weren't sure what we were asking for but certainly to ask for safety and protection for Guy and peace for us as we waited.

I went to work as usual. I took the train to Newark, and then the path train from there, to 1 WTC. I sat at my desk, on the 78th floor. It overlooks midtown Manhattan. Two coworkers came in early. Our boss wasn't in yet for our morning meeting so we jointly decided to have breakfast. We went down to the cafeteria on the 43rd floor. I just sat down to eat my granola and drink my Diet Pepsi when suddenly our world changed.

The building started to move and we heard an explosion. It felt like the building was going to topple over it moved so much. We all looked at each other trying to think of some explanation. I reacted by grabbing the table we were seated at with both hands. It swayed back and forth and then finally came to rest. Once the building stabilized, we looked out the window and saw debris; papers and such began to fall. We moved to the center of the cafeteria, to keep away from the glass, and wait for some announcement, although none would come. All the drills, all the tests of the system, all the emergency systems failed just when we needed it most. At this point, we knew it was bad, really bad.

I dropped to my knees and began to pray. I asked God to spare us, guide us and use me in the situation to the best of my ability. A maintenance worker listened to his radio and just shouted to head down the stairs. Not feeling the need to be told twice we moved. But where were the stairs? I know why they tell you to look for exits before an accident. They are harder to find during an emergency. They were actually right under our noses. My wife would tell you of course, that is where everything is that I can't find.

My one coworker led the way. It was funny to see him hesitate when opening the fire exit only doors. The door was labeled, "alarm will sound." I guess it just intimidated him or maybe the realization of it all set in. Once the door was opened we saw that there were people in the stairs already.

Once on the stairs, there was a sense of relief. Just walking down the stairs made me feel better. The helpless feeling of grabbing a table when a 110-story building feels like it will topple cannot be described. Doing something proactive was good and part of my nature.

The exit began orderly and ended that way. There was no great sense of panic. It's just that we all wanted to get down. We thought it would be safe down there. The woman behind me began to get hysterical. I asked what was wrong. She stated she was claustrophobic. I just started to talk to her telling her we have been spared and need to just get down and out of the building.

At each floor I counted out loud in order to bring comfort to her and myself. Each floor meant we were closer to our rescue. Smoke began filtering into the stairs. They had not shut down the air system yet. The smoke burned our eyes, lips, and mouth. But thank God we were alive.

Around the 36th floor another woman began to wheeze. I asked her what was wrong and she told me that she was asthmatic. A man offered her his inhaler, which she used but continued to struggle. I was now talking with both women trying to keep them calm and engaged so they wouldn't have time to let their minds work against them.

As I said, there was no panic. But there were very nervous people. One woman kept yelling out "keep it moving." Now why didn't we think of that, I thought. But as people entered the stairs we had to wait. I guess that is the luxury of being on the lower floors.

Around the 20th floor, we passed a man in a wheelchair. Another man and I offered to take him down. He said no, he would wait. I think he knew he would tie up the stairs. All I could think was what a self-sacrifice.

On the 14th floor we had to stop to allow a fireman to pass as he walked up. It was now about 100 degrees, with stale air. They turned off the vents or their failure kept the smoke from getting worse. But here we were, 14 floors to our rescue and he had 66 + to his destination. He had on full gear, oxygen tank, hats, suits and jacket. His face will always remain in my mind, and his family will remain in my prayers.

Around the 10th floor, we passed a small group with one woman who was having trouble. I assumed it was breathing difficulties. She had plenty of people with her so there was nothing to do.

On the 6th floor, things seemed to worsen. Water was pouring into the staircase. There were little waterfalls off each stair. It made the trip down more cautious. My conversations with these two women continued. I guess in the end keeping them calm kept me calm. Somewhere after the 10th floor there were people trying to listen to the radio. Bits and pieces of what happened were floating up and down the staircase.

The doorbell rang several more times. Another neighbor, my Mom, and a woman from church were here. I told one of the women that until I hear otherwise I will believe that Guy is okay. I also told her that I didn't want to live without him. But the fears crept in. What if he wasn't okay, what if he didn't make it out, what if he were hurt, injured or unconscious. What was he going through? Was he stuck in a room somewhere unable to escape? Trapped on the stairs, or worse, was he in his office with his back to the plane as it plunged through the glass. Why didn't the news show if people even were able to escape from the building? Logically, it didn't seem feasible. Would anyone even have been able to make it outside in such a short period of time? If they did, surely the news cameras would be all over them. Yet it eerily didn't show anyone walking out. What if they were in the elevators when all this happened? What if they are stuck in a stairwell? I was unable to continue my thoughts of horror because they were interrupted by more phone calls.

Thoughts of living without him entered my mind. I will never talk to him at work, I will never tell him about what's happening on the farm, or what the boys are doing today. I longed to hear his voice. I longed to see his handsome face. I thought about being a widow. I thought about the boys without their Dad. I thought, how could I live without him. How could I go on even another day without knowing that he will walk through the doors at 7:30 every evening. How I wanted to savor every little detail of every day that I used to take for granted.

I shook my head and thought no. God is with him. A peace came over me just then, and my neighbor came into the kitchen with a look on her face that I'll never forget,

she asked, "what building is Guy in?"

"Building one," I said.

"Oh Vicky, Bldg. 1 just collapsed."

It was then that the peace left me, how in the world could anyone survive now? There didn't seem to have been enough time to be evacuated and directed to safety. Even if they had made it onto the street, the collapse of the tower would guarantee death of those standing outside. Suddenly I felt all alone, everyone and everything melted away. It was as if I traveled through space and time to find myself standing in the throne room with God. Only one other time did I experience this feeling in my life. It was about a year earlier. We had just purchased this farm. My son contracted Lyme's disease at the age of fourteen. It was such a rare form of it that resulted in first degree heart block. Only 1% of people get this strain. He was put into intensive care. The doctors told me that if we didn't hospitalize him immediately we would lose him. Outwardly, he seemed perfectly healthy to me. Inwardly he was fighting a battle for his life. I went to the chapel in the hospital and dropped to my knees sobbing hysterically. It was then that I found myself kneeling before God, imploring Him to spare my son's life. He did. I now found myself pleading once again in front of the mighty King for my husband's life. Nothing was real except for His presence as I prayed for my husband. Once again we were facing low percentages. It isn't everyday that a terrorist group fly a plane into someone's workplace. Again, I begged God to beat the odds.

People were looking at me with despair, with that look of "you poor widow". I insisted that I am not going to assume my husband is dead. Just because there is a plane with a lot of fuel that exploded into a skyscraper didn't mean we had to be pessimistic. My company looked at me as if I were in denial. My neighbor came back in and said it was bldg. 2 that had collapsed. I thought "Oh thank God" realizing how utterly selfish I was at this moment. It was at this point that I collapsed onto the kitchen floor with tears of relief and hope. Maybe there was a chance that he still can make it out of the building and get far away from the area I thought. Meanwhile the reports kept coming in. We were now aware of the attack on the Pentagon. Within moments we heard the report about the plane that went down in Pennsylvania. "Oh Lord, what is happening? What else? There was an anxious feeling of foreboding. Are the bridges in danger? Are the tunnels safe? So much has happened in such a short time that our minds just can't fathom the magnitude of what this means. I fought the panic that was in my heart. Helplessness is overwhelming, there's nothing to do but wait, and wait. "Tower One is going down" the newscaster screeched. A sound so awful to bear. "Oh no, not my husband's building. Run Guy Run."

When we reached the ground floor and could see outside we knew how bad it was. Explosions, fires, and glass were everywhere outside the building. The lobby was a mess but intact, and empty except for a line of people making their way out. A rescue worker stopped me and asked what floor we were from and what the conditions were. I gave him my report. As we began our journey out, things worsened. It is impossible to explain the amount of devastation your eyes can hold. Pictures cannot capture it. It is the smell of smoke, the cries and tears, fire, chaos, and the smell of the death in the air.

Here one of my collegues had separated from us. We were ushered out by security personnel, through the main lobby, through a water shower from the fire sprinklers. It was refreshing after our long trip down. We made our way into the Trade Center mall. I heard small explosions intermittently. It would be months before I realized it was the sound of bodies hitting the pavement. We were led down and out toward Broadway. Once we got out, we were told to stay under the overhang, turn off cell phones, and don't look up. So we looked up. My heart sank. I knew I cheated death. I knew I was alive and anyone in our office was not going to be able to survive from what I could see from the ground. Where our offices were, was now replaced by a gaping hole where the plane had entered the building. Fire and smoke were everywhere.

A woman started to scream hysterically and ran towards us. She was reaching out for anyone to catch her. I caught her, and she cried as we continued to walk, I lost track of the other two women from the stairs. When we made it to Broadway, the woman let go and walked away.

So many times that morning we offered up prayers. It seemed to be impossible to save Guy. It seemed too late. Yet the Scriptures echoed in my mind. Jesus looked at them and said, "With man this is impossible, but with God all things are possible."

Matthew 19:25-27 Against all the odds, we continued to pray remembering that God IS timeless. Common sense told me it was too late to pray. But the Holy Spirit told me, it is never too late to pray. God is already on the move for His beloved children knowing the desires of their heart before they even know what their needs are. It was time to fully trust in Him.

I thought, Lord, I don't know what the end result of today will be but you do. I am trusting you. No matter what happens, I am trusting in you. I realize that I may already be a widow and the only way that my children and I can face tomorrow, or even tonight, would be with your hand upon us for without you Lord this is too much to bear.

A silence enveloped the room as we stared blankly at the news. It was as if we waited for them to say this has all been a mistake. But we watched over and over again as the plane hit the building. I looked around the room. Everything was still. Even my parrots were quiet. As I looked around, I noticed how dirty the room was. I looked to see if anyone else noticed. "Gee, if I knew there would be a terrorist attack today, I would have cleaned my house." I said rather apologetically. Realizing now that if they didn't notice the mess I have certainly brought it to their attention.

I kept envisioning Guy's car in the driveway. He would burst through the door, run to me, wipe away my tears, and all would once again be right with the world. I thought of all the silliness I had expressed through the years. How our minds let us fester small idiosyncracies. How embarrassed I would be when he asked why I kicked him under the table or when I asked him to lower his voice because he was too loud or the feeling of annoyance that his laundry sat on the floor right in front of the hamper instead of in it. How many times I had been aggravated by this. I would think, 'is it so much to ask that when you are in the vicinity of the hamper that you actually put a little extra effort and open the lid?' Now I longed to see his clothes from today laying in front of the hamper where I can see them. Indicating to me that this was all over and he was safe.

As you go through a crisis, thoughts are dichotomous. They range from rational thoughts pertaining to the crisis to such random, left field thoughts. I was having a plethora of them. They would swirl in my mind relooping just as the news reel kept cruelly relooping the planes crashing into the towers. Each time I saw the film footage my mind would think maybe this time it won't crash.

Tolyk, my youngest son, called from school wanting to know if I had heard from Dad. I tried to reassure him that although we don't know anything yet, that I am sure he is fine and I will call him soon as I hear. We both tried to be strong and hung up the phone. My poor child was scared and anxious; I could hear it in his voice. How will he ever be able to deal with this? I wondered if his faith was strong enough to carry him through. I wanted to pick him up from school but was afraid to leave the television and the phone. Suddenly building one collapsed. Now, both buildings were down. Gripping horror set in at the same time bewilderment that the towers didn't just topple over bringing blocks and blocks of devastation upon New York City. There was no longer any misunderstanding of the events. Hope was but a faint flicker. Did anyone make it out of the buildings in time? There was no sign of people leaving the building on the news. Even if they did get out, surely the buildings collapsing would have killed them all because there hadn't been enough time. Back and forth my mind went. Fear for myself, my children, for Guy. I wished that we could connect on some level. I wanted to comfort him and then prayed so hard that God would let Guy feel His hand on him. Yet, there was a peace that came over me which I didn't quite understand.

On Broadway there was a small church. I had to stop and pray. I got on my knees and thanked Him for sparing me. It was then I got an overwhelming urge to go home. My colleague and I kept walking, we knew we had to get to a phone but I wanted to get out of NYC. The phone lines were long. I felt urged to head north up Broadway. Somehow the two women from the stairwell found us again and thanked me. I just asked them to thank God and go home now.

A cab had just emptied out in front of us so we jumped in and we started our journey to Penn Station. The radio was on and all the reports were coming in. I was in a state of shock. It all seemed so unreal and that this would be over soon. But things worsened once again in the safety of our cab now 10 blocks away, the WTC 2 fell. My heart sank, my thoughts were of the firemen we saw in the building and how many were still in the one tower. That urge to get out saved my life again had we stayed; we very well could have been piled under WTC 2.

We got out of the cab, my legs finally showed signs of weakness, and sharp pain. I headed into a store, an art gallery I think. I asked to use the phone. I tried to call home but the phone would not connect. I then called my NJ office and asked to speak with my boss. I told him our brief story and begged him to call home. We found out that everyone from our office was accounted for and safe. I tried to call home again, this time the phone rang.

Suddenly, the phone rang, looking at the caller ID, it said NEW YORK and a number I didn't recognize. Two thoughts crossed my mind, Oh, God, this is the worst call of my life or Oh Thank God, this is the best call of my life! I yelled it's New York, and with much trepidation answered it, and heard Guy's voice on the other. I yelled Honey and fell again to my knees, this time unable to control the heavy sobs that had welted up inside of me for three hours. Without saying another word, we both just cried into the phone for what seemed like an eternity. For three hours I pondered his fate. For three hours, although there were people here, I was alone, faced with the possibility that I will be going to bed alone for the rest of my life. After about 5 minutes, it occurred to me to ask, "Are you all-right?" "Are you hurt?"

"I'm fine, just very shaken up."

"Get away from the building." I gasped realizing he may still be in harm's way.

"I'm not near the sight anymore. I'm going to try to get out of the city."

"I love you and I'm so glad you are okay."

"Me too. I love you. Bye." Meanwhile everyone in the family room had screamed and were crying and giving praises to God for answering our prayers.

After the call, we walked over to Penn Station. It was still open. I got on the concourse and said goodbye to my coworker. Trains were running. Mine was just called.

I quickly got on it, and actually got a seat as the train filled up. Then an announcement came that they were closing the station. The conductor asked us to detrain. Being too tired and with nowhere to go, I stayed. The train was just about empty when the announcement was made that we could go, the train refilled quickly. Then once again the announcement came to detrain.

I had nowhere to go and little strength to go there. Sitting on this train made more sense, sooner or later it was going to go to NJ. I wanted to make sure I was on it. A few people stayed also. Then with the train less than a third filled, it left. I was on my way home.

Once at the train station in NJ, I called Vicky and asked her to pick me up and bring my car keys since mine were left beside my desk. She came, we embraced, politely rejected to be interviewed by a local reporter and went home.

Everyone left except my Mom. Just then a mutual friend of ours, , showed up at the door with a grief stricken face. I met him at the door with the good news followed by an embrace and he broke down sobbing. My Mom made him sit in the chair to compose himself.

I called the school and when asked for Tolyk, the secretary just said, "Thank God you called" The principal got on the phone and asked if everything was all-right as well as the secretary. I left word to have Tolyk and DJ paged and have them call back

Tolyk called back and I told him. He was relieved but wanted to get off the phone. DJ called. He too was relieved but told me that Tolyk wanted to go home, but he didn't. He needed to stay and keep his mind off of the events. Thoughts of being fatherless had entered his mind; thoughts that he would be the man of the house and have to pull it together for us emotionally and financially crept into his thinking, responsibility unbelievable for a 16 year old to have. Our friend jumped into the car to get Tolyk. He met him at the school and embraced him. When Tolyk got home he hugged us and voluntarily went out to take care of the farm animals who had not been fed yet. About two, Guy called and said he was at the train station and for me to bring his keys. My body trembled involuntarily. My legs were like rubber. I could barely walk let alone drive so once again our friend offered to take me to the train station. When I got there I ran to Guy unable to control my tears along the way. We both cried. We both held on tightly. A reporter wanted an interview which Guy declined. And then we drove home.

We all went out to dinner that evening to get away from the phones and news. We ended up in a restaurant that had many televisions all broadcasting the events. Oh well. When we returned home we were greeted with many more phone calls and people stopping in to see if Guy had survived.

About 6 months ago we had ordered landscaping rocks for our garden. The man who delivered the rocks remembered that Guy worked at the trade center and called to see if he was safe. We were so touched by this genuine concern from a virtual stranger.

A woman from our church pulled up in the driveway . She delivered a meal for us. She also wanted to check and see if we had heard from Guy. I filled her in on the sequence of events and then I told her that I was starting up a bible study two weeks from tonight.

I watched some of the news that night. There was a small story about a van that was found on the GW Bridge in NY with explosives. They were trying to blow up the bridges too?! The goal was to completely isolate NYC. The hospitals were geared up for thousands of casualties and triage patients. Over 7,000 body bags were ordered that day.

Sleeping that night was futile. I tossed all night. I would close my eyes and relive the day. I would open my eyes and relive the day. I felt an overwhelming sense of sadness. Although I felt extremely grateful for my husband's life, I, like most Americans, was staring at an act of war on US soil for the first time in my life. I felt so insecure. I knew in my heart that nothing would ever be the same.

I would like to say that our story ended that night but little did we know, it had just begun.

Chapter Two
In the Wake

The days blurred for a while. There was a numbing feeling. We felt like we were living zombies. By the 13th we were feeling so helpless and victimized. Although I felt a tremendous relief that God had spared Guy's life, watching him relive the moments was horrific. I didn't know how to make it better for my husband. I then remembered how he had always said that in a crisis you can either be paralyzed or proactive. I decided we needed to be proactive. I asked him if he wanted to go and help with the search efforts. He said he couldn't handle it. I then suggested we do the next best thing. Let's go and raise money for the victims and their families. We quickly called around for a public place to hold this mini fundraiser. After a few rejections, our local WAWA generously offered to let us use their parking lot and that they would post the signs on their windows. We scheduled it for the next day. We also called a local church and asked Pastor John Grove to join us for a candlelight vigil and prayer. We decided to raise the money specifically for the Fireman's Widow Fund. We stood outside in the parking lot from 4-7pm. We handed out bibles, tracts, and Guy's testimony about 9/11. At 6:00 we had a small prayer service. No one was around for this. I felt disappointed. Then one by one, the employees of the WAWA came out to join us. Tears welled up in our eyes as well as in the employees' eyes. We cried out to God. We cried for the families of those missing or killed. We cried out for our country. We cried out for our President and the enormous task ahead of him. We thanked the Lord for being in control and that although we didn't comprehend what was happening, we knew that God did and would turn this around to His glory. At 7:00 we packed up and counted the money. We had raised $500.00 in 3 hours .

Guy had stayed home from work for two weeks. His company had a New Jersey office that he could report to, but he just couldn't bring himself to get up and go. Our Pastor, Joe Olechea, had come by that first week nearly every day just to sit and talk with Guy and pray with him. CBN News had contacted us. They had heard of Guy's testimony. They setup an interview with us in our home. We had to re-enact the reactions of that day. It wasn't hard. As we sat here pretending to watch the towers fall on t.v. , it was right there in my mind's eye. I saw the whole thing all over again even though the television was off. I had wondered how we could do a re-enactment without seeming phony. It wasn't phony. It just happened. All of us in the room relived the day as if it were just happening. After the interview, I felt drained. The emotions were still too fresh and raw.

On September 25, 2001, I had started a bible study in my home with 5 other women. We were using "Experiencing God" by Henry Blackwell. This became such a profound study for all of us but especially for me. Experiencing God, discusses learning to listen to God. It explores understanding that God's will is perfect and that we need to line up our will with his. In one of the chapters, Henry Blackwell explains how to draw closer to God. When you don't, God does allow crisis to come to bring you into a more intimate relationship with him. I was able to relate to this, point by point.

Guy was very restless. We decided to remodel the kitchen. I didn't complain. I knew he needed to do some busy work and the kitchen just seemed to lend itself for the job. And oh yes, I did manage to burn the counter top with a glass candle holder just as he was trying to figure out what to do with himself.

Every morning I would check all the major new stations. There was an impending feeling of foreboding. I felt an anticipation for the other shoe to drop; a sense that something far worse would soon happen. The news had been reporting war, and rumors of war. We had confirmation via a video tape that Osama Bin Laden was in fact responsible for the attack on the World Trade Center, Flight 93, and the Pentagon.

Everywhere we went people were talking about 9/11. There was no escaping it. Patriotism replaced cynicism. Flags donned cars, barns, houses, and stores. Signs toting "In God we trust" or "God bless America" adorned the streets. I wondered if it adorned our hearts? Church attendance was up. Everyone was looking for an answer. Would it be short lived? Once we settled back into our routines as a nation would we dismiss God once again? Do we need to live in a constant state of fear in order to seek God or would we now stay on the straight and narrow road.

Everyone we met wanted to know Guy's story. We recapped it time and time again. My brother shared the story with his neighbor. Sometime later, maybe a few weeks after 911, she called my brother. She informed him that there was an article in the paper that was specifically addressed to Guy. It was a thank you from one of the women that he had helped in Tower One. In the article, she profusely thanked him and called him an angel. She also said that her family was appreciative that he helped her or they wouldn't be with her today if not for him. His neighbor mailed the article to Guy. Guy was very humbled by it and even somewhat embarrassed since he did what he thought was right and didn't feel he deserved any fanfare for it.

On October 7, 2001, we went to church since it was Sunday. Immediately following the service, we had a church luncheon. As Pastor Joe came to lead us in prayer before eating, he announced, "Ladies and gentlemen, the US has just declared war on Afghanistan. Let's bow our heads in pray." The room filled with gasps and tears. It was happening. There were concerns of retaliation. There were concerns for our troops. Our 18year old soldiers suddenly seemed much too young to be sent into war. We prayed and prayed.

I decided we needed a safe room. It would have to be nuclear resistant and have enough food for six months supply. I gathered up shovels and searched the Red Cross' website for information on putting together a disaster kit. I stocked up on water and canned food. This was a good time to get the kids to eat the vegetables they hated. I was ready. I also mapped out an escape route in case of an attack on a nuclear plant. This was serious. I was very serious. I even thought of buying a gun. I thought about taking my kids out of school. I thought about how I never had to think about this before. I wanted to feel in control. I wanted to never be unprepared for another sneak attack again. All of my planning didn't give me a piece of mind. So I took out my bible and read:

Psalm 46,

1"God is our refuge and strength,
an ever-present help in trouble.

2 Therefore we will not fear, though the earth give
way and the mountains fall into the heart of the
sea,

3 though its waters roar and foam
and the mountains quake with their surging."

God was in control even on September 11th. He is our refuge. The news was reporting that the death toll was dropping from the original count.

Several weeks have gone by. Guy is experiencing chest pains as well as shortness of breath. He was working in the New Jersey office now. It was setup for only 12 employees and now had 24. Everyone shared a desk, a phone, and a computer. This only increased his anxiety. As he read through e-mails at work, they were addressed to him or to whomever was reading this on his behalf.

Finally his chest pains got the best of him so he went to the doctor. The doctor suggested taking anti-anxiety medicine that perhaps he was experiencing Post Traumatic Stress Disorder (PTSD). As a precaution, the doctor wanted him to go for an x-ray. He was having nightmares each night. He was extremely depressed during the day. I would search out as many humorous farm events as I could to add levity, to create a distraction, to give him something to focus on. I tried to be upbeat all the time. I asked the children not bother him with questions and above all else don't bicker in front of him--for their sake.

I would find refuge on the farm. When no one was home I would lean on the fence and just cry into the night. My mind still couldn't wrap itself around what had happened and what was in store for our country. I cried because our lives were affected down to our souls. Although Guy had survived, we were in mourning. Grieving for life the way it used to be in our home. Lamenting life the way it was in the US. I cried for myself. I felt forgotten. I felt my shoulders just couldn't keep carrying my whole family. I was wearing a plastic smile. No one was concerned how this was all affecting me. The questions were directed to Guy as people discovered that he had been in the World Trade Center. That was okay. Yet, I felt like I was on the outside looking in and that I really didn't have a right to be affected. The ironic part is that I wasn't so upset because of the World Trade Center. I did feel I could count my blessings for that. Rather, it was the aftermath, the effects on my husband. It was the oppressing cloud that hung over the country, the anger that filled my younger son rendering him unreachable. I began dreaming of a simpler time. Reminiscing of my childhood when I had no worries, when my family was intact, and if there was anything wrong, Mom & Dad would fix it. I wanted them to fix this.

I spent a lot of time out in the barnyard with the animals. Observing them playing and grazing. They had no worries. They were pretty certain that at 6:00, I would provide food, water, and shelter. How sure were they? I wasn't sure. My mind was distracted these days. Yet, I would feed them every night at 6:00 and every morning. Then it hit me! They had more faith in me, than I had in God! God was providing for us, spiritually, physically, and emotionally. Yet, I didn't really trust it.

Sadness and frustration found expression in me from time to time. Once again, I was rather peaceful. It was surreal. I called our former pastor and friend, Tim Chicola, from North Jersey and asked him if I were in denial or was this the peace that transcends all understanding. The trust was I didn't understand it. He said that it wasn't denial because I am acknowledging what has happened. It was the peace that passes all understanding. He further explained, much to my chagrin, that my personality wasn't characteristically calm. That wasn't my style. After knowing me for years, he knows how I react to things. So as not to prove him right, I refrained from commenting on that. Therefore, he said, the peace was coming from God. It was strange. I almost tried to fight the peace thinking that this was not practical. Hard as I would try, the peace enveloped me. It was almost euphoric.

Guy and I had a long talk. We discussed how people would be watching us to see how we handle all of it. Our unsaved friends and family will be scrutinizing us to see if we are acting like Christians. It's easy to act like a Christian when all is going well. The true test of Christian values is when you walk through the valley. We knew that even our "Christian" brothers and sisters would be watching us and evaluating just how spiritual we are depending on how we handle ourselves.

The next day, the school called me. Tolyk had been attacked in the cafeteria by another student. Guy was home that day so we both drove over to the school. We sat in the principal's office as he explained that as the students came off the bus, they enter through the cafeteria. As Tolyk was walking, a boy jumped him from behind and began beating on him. Tolyk just stood there and told him he wasn't going to hit him back. At this point the boy kept punching him. My other son was walking past and yelled at the boy to get off his brother. That's when it stopped. Tolyk was crumpled onto the floor after having been pushed over a lunch table. He felt a bit dazed and dizzy.

After a long discussion with the principal, he called the local police and we went down and filed a complaint. We asked Tolyk why this happened. He said, "About three weeks ago they were on the bus. We'll call this boy Tom, Tom was always cursing and threatening people. He had been expelled from his last school and his parents had shipped him off to live with his grandparents in our town. Well, this one day on the bus, everyone was throwing papers and Tolyk hit Tom with one of these pieces of paper. Tom told him he would get him one day for this. For three weeks he had premeditated his attack. He would terrorize Tolyk at school with threats and finally the day came that he carried out his plans. To us, it was an act of terrorism once again. Tolyk, who had been angry since 9/11, had just undergone his own nightmare.

We were afraid for his safety, especially since we pressed charges but knew that it had to be done. We also realized that our son took ridicule, abuse, beatings, and torment. It brought to mind, our Lord and Savior Jesus Christ. For a moment, we understood. Jesus had been blameless. He knew what he stood for and did not waiver. He didn't change just because he was being persecuted. He endured but not for his own sake but for ours. He suffered for our sake, he even suffered for Tom's sake. Tolyk didn't deserve what Tom did to him. Jesus, didn't deserve what was done to him but he did it out of incredible love for us. I heard a pastor ask his congregation, "How many of you believe that God loves us because Jesus died on the cross?" Many raised their hands. He said, "No, that's incorrect. Jesus died on the cross because God loves us." A subtle but significant difference.

Guy became worse with each day. Finally I sat him down lovingly and said, "Honey, the doctor gave you medicine to take the edge off. Either you take the medicine or I will but one of us needs to be medicated!" He started to laugh.

Guy was ready to go for his chest x-ray. A week went by before we heard anything. We received a phone call from the doctor's office who said that there was a growth on his heart. He wanted him to go for an echo cardiogram and a stress test. We called our insurance company to find out which facility was covered. We discovered, that the insurance had been cancelled by Guy's employer. This was just unbelievable. We knew he needed the procedure done but we couldn't afford it on our own. He called his employer who assured him that one way or another, he would make sure that the bill would be paid. We set up the appointment. It would be two weeks before we could have the tests done. So we waited. Sometimes not knowing what you are dealing with is worse than knowing and confronting the problem.

Finally the day came and we went to the cardiology center and had the procedure done. It took several hours but afterward the cardiologist came out and spoke with us. The growth on his heart is a cyst. It is most likely congenital and of no consequence. The stress test was fine and barring another plane flying into his building, he should live a long healthy life.

It had been nearly three months since that attack. We now knew that Guy was experiencing PTSD, survivor's guilt, and was having anxiety attacks. He still refused to take his medicine. But now that we knew his lungs were clear and his heart was in good shape, some of the anxiety had subsided. It had been that the more his chest hurt, the more nervous he had become that he had inhaled some chemical on 9/11, the more his chest hurt. Scripture tells us to be anxious for nothing. Now it was time to put that into practice.

Paychecks had been coming late. Although they were due on the 15th and 30th of each month, they would typically be two weeks later than the pay date. Around the first week of December, Guy came home from work upset. "They have suspended pay until further notice." We were suddenly faced with a new level of problems as a result of the terrorist attack—financial problems with no preparation. Christmas was right around the corner and of course, so were all of our monthly bills. A panic crept into my heart. What were we going to do now.

The latest on the news was the mishandling of blood by the Red Cross and money that had been donated had been rerouted to various different organizations other than for the 9/11 fund. The president of the Red Cross stepped down. This was such a shame. All those people who had stood on long lines to give their blood and now it was contaminated because they didn't refrigerate it. What about all those donations. People thought they were donating to the 9/11 fund. It shouldn't go anywhere else. It was an outrage. It seemed like everyone was going mad. Perhaps we were leading that procession.

Christmas was modest but beautiful. We weren't really in the mood to celebrate but despite ourselves had a blessed holy day (or holiday-as I prefer the first). January rolled around and Pastor Tim called us. Several years ago we had started a computer ministry at his church. It was free and opened to the public. Its purpose was to take the intimidation out of learning computers and to give a skill to those who need it. People are usually afraid to take a class on technical topics because the costs are so high and if they don't do well they have spent a lot of money which they may not have. When money is no longer an issue, people are willing to risk failure. As it turned out, everyone we encountered succeeded. Tim was cleaning out the computer room and asked if we were planning to continue the ministry in South Jersey. We hadn't thought much about it but decided it's probably a good time to start. He offered us the equipment that we had left behind however we needed to remove it soon since they needed the room for something else.

We went up and loaded the car on two different occasions. Guy then unloaded all the equipment in our already overcrowded garage. He spent hours repairing and rebuilding the machines. After several weekend's worth of work, he had all the machines up and running. He then went to speak with the pastor at our church. After explaining what our ministry was all about and how former students had improved their job situations, gained self-confidence, and two had started attending church, Pastor Joe said he thinks it's an exciting ministry but needs to discuss it with the deacons.

January also brought with it a month's worth of bills. We didn't have enough money left to pay each bill in its entirety especially the credit cards. I began calling and asking if I could make a smaller payment than the minimum due. They told me no. I could still send a smaller amount but then I would be subjected to a late fee on the amount I didn't pay and then this would bring the percentage up to the maximum. In most cases this was about 25% finance charge. I was aghast.

I paid off as much as I could and then I called the finance companies on our cars in order to defer payments. We had three cars financed because we had purchased a car for my Mom a few years ago. Two finance companies were great and deferred payments for two months billing us only for the interest for those two months. When I called the third finance company to inform them we were going to be late (for the first time) on our payment and that I wanted to defer payment, the woman on the other end of the phone began questioning me. What was the reason? Why can't I find money to pay? Where is the car now? What condition is it in? What is the mileage? I stopped her and asked why all these questions? She informed me that she needed this information to repossess my car. But why, I am not in default of my loan, and I called you in good faith to tell you that the payment would be late and to see if we could arrange a deferment program. She told me that I would have to be current on my loan before she would entertain any special program.

Her tone was so accusatory. I felt worse than a beggar. I felt like a criminal. I hung up the phone crying and then my husband called the headquarters. He immediately called the vice president of the company who then called me to apologize and setup a payment plan that would be conducive to our situation.

We were put on the prayer request list at church. The next day a woman showed up with bags and bags of groceries. I insisted we weren't that desperate yet. She insisted I take the groceries and to let her bless me. I graciously accepted but still thought it wasn't necessary. I could still feed my family and I certainly had enough food in my cabinets. The next Sunday, someone handed me gift certificates for a supermarket from an anonymous person. I thought this was premature, we weren't destitute yet.

A deacon approached Guy and handed him an envelope. Guy handed back the envelope and told him to go and speak to me. As he walked toward me I knew something was up. My heart began to race. I wasn't used to having to reject people and I wasn't used to accepting gifts. The deacon told me that the deacon board had written a check for us from the benevolent fund. I thanked him and said, "We really appreciate this. But please save it for someone who needs it. We are okay. We really are. Guy's boss had said that pay should be reinstated by the end of January." On the way home from church Guy asked, "Did the deacon talk to you?"

"Yes. He wanted to give me a check but I told him we didn't need it."

"I told him the same thing." Guy said.

"Why did we do that? We really could use the money."

Yeah I know. But it's my job to provide for my family though."

It was at this point that God hit me over the head. He made me realize that we did need the money and our refusal was pride. Pride, I thought. I'm not prideful. I had always prided myself on being humble for goodness sakes. Yet I couldn't dismiss this thought. Pride huh? I don't think so. Then I thought about it some more. We needed the money. Our situation was a difficult one. We had no means to pay any more bills. Someone had just offered us money as a gift. Why then did we refuse? It occurred to me that I didn't want to be viewed as needy.

We were always the ones who tried to help other people. We always treated people for dinner. I didn't want to admit that this situation had changed. I didn't want to acknowledge that we needed help. It wasn't our style. We were not the type of people to be in need. What does that boil down to? Pride. Plain and simple. I could justify my reasoning. I could say we were just being polite. But the bottom line was that pride stood between us and that check. I wanted to be a giver not a receiver. Why? Yes, because my pride wanted to see me that way. I was brought to my knees. Oh Lord, we are prideful. We refused to receive charity because it insulted us. We weren't living on the street and therefore felt above a handout. Oh Lord I cried, let my pride fall down. And that was exactly what he was about to do.

Chapter Three
Humbled

I suddenly became very popular. The phone rang off the hook. No it wasn't people from church checking on us nor was it a neighbor calling to say hi. It was a borage of bill collectors. I was interrogated by someone who wanted to know why my husband wasn't looking for another job. They wanted to know how much my husband gets paid. I said right now, nothing.

"You have always been a preferred customer. I can see by our records that you have always paid above the minimum due. We would hate to see your credit affected by this."

"Oh is there something we can work out temporarily?" I asked feeling a little hopeful.

"Well we can offer you to pay by phone free of charge."

My sarcastic side wanted to ask if I could use my credit card but I refrained. I said, "Don't you understand that there isn't any money. My husband was involved in the World Trade Center disaster and as a result has not been paid since December. Is there any way we can suspend payment with a promissary note to pay in a month or two?"

"No ma'am when do you think you will be sending in your payment?"

"Well, I'm praying about it and will let you know as soon as I receive an answer. Goodbye."

Another credit card company asked, "Why aren't you sending a payment this month?" I again went through the WTC rhetoric .

"Did you know your husband wouldn't be paid?"

"No."

"When did you find out that his pay was suspended?"

"December."

"Then why did you keep charging on your account?"

"I didn't. As long as I was able to pay monthly, I was still using my card. But if you check your records you will see that there were no purchases made in December or January."

"Do you work?"

"No."

"Why not? Don't you think you should be helping your husband?"

"I will send a check as soon as I am able. Goodbye."

I was devastated. I felt like a criminal. I was being treated like a societal outcast. I spared Guy all the nonsense and didn't share with him the borage of phone calls I would receive weekly. Where was the compassion and understanding of yesteryear. Where there still remained a human touch. One could explain a situation and the other person had sympathy. They really did give extensions and deferments. Where were the bank owners like George Bailey on It's a Wonderful Life? We are so computerized that we no longer deal with people as humans. I was not a preferred customer. I wasn't even a customer. I was a dollar sign and now I was a minus sign. I had fear that we would lose our home. My mother, who came from behind the iron curtain, had had her home taken away by the communists twice. I grew up listening to the tragedy my mother had experienced and now was afraid that this was happening to me. I glanced out the window. Just then a chicken ran across the yard. This was a common sight yet, for the first time since moving here, it was so precious to me. Everything that I had taken for granted up to this point was special. I was experiencing a deep appreciation for everything I was now in danger of losing. My pride was starting to fall for reasons beyond my control.

Pastor Joe approached us one day after services about the computer ministry. He had spoken with the deacons and they had some concerns. They had very limited space and the computers would have to be taken down after every class and stored away until the next class since that room was used for children's church. Guy said that's fine. Pastor Joe said he will bring it up again with the deacons and get back to us.

Meanwhile, Guy, along with coworkers, went into Manhattan to seek assistance from Safe Horizons which was coordinating all assistance from various organizations. Upon arriving at the center, they had to be assigned a number. Then they were shuffled onto a bus to wait. After several hours, they were then brought in to be interviewed. After spending much time rehashing the events, providing documentation, and many emotions, they were then sent to another room (to another organization) and had to do it again. Afterwards, they went to yet another room, went through the same drill, and then had to wait for a decision.

A few hours later, those approved were issued checks for assistance. Guy arrived home fatigued, humbled, and depressed. The assistance was quite a blessing but he felt like a beggar and reliving everything again was just too much for his close to the edge nerves. He retired early that night. It would take several days before he could snap out of it. For all the negative press the Red Cross had received, they were extremely helpful to us and the folks that had been interviewed. Our bills were taken care of for three months except for our credit card bills.

In February the phone calls from credit card companies began again. This time however, we owed more money than we did in January due to late charge and an increase in the finance charge percentage. Again I told them that I was praying and would get back to them.

I submitted. In an act of desperation I again went on my knees and surrendered my pride to the Lord. I realized that it all belonged to the Lord anyway. None of it was ever mine. It had always belonged to him. Even the sheep and cattle on the hills were His and we were just stewards. Perhaps I hadn't been a good steward. I had always thought that these things belonged to me and that I had earned them. Humbling, very humbling.

The phone calls became a weekly event. The ringing would frighten me. Caller ID was of no help since it usually only read "unknown caller" which included people I know. I dreaded answering the phone. I decided to call several debt consolidation companies. After spending a grueling 20 minutes on each answering questions they said,

"I'm sorry but we will not be able to help you since you're husband is not working."

"But he is working. It's just that his pay has been suspended temporarily."

"I'm sorry Ma'am but unless he is receiving a steady paycheck of any amount we cannot do anything for you." Another dead end what were we going to do? There were no options left. Panic gripped my heart.

Then I made a daring phone call. I called a Christian radio station which airs a program called "Money Matters" with Larry Burkett. I got on the air and had 45 seconds. I summarized our situation and asked if we had any other options other than declaring bankruptcy for our credit cards. Larry had provided me with the name of a financial planner and a debt consolidation company. I already knew that they wouldn't be able to help me and feeling very discouraged, I thanked him hung up the phone. A short time later, a gentleman from the studio called and asked if I had listened to the rest of the broadcast. I said no.

He said, "Oh that's too bad. During the commercial break, Larry felt God had put your situation on his heart and after getting back on the air did something very unusual. He announced that he was going to contribute money and encouraged the listening audience to do the same if they felt led. The operators were standing by to take those calls." I was overwhelmed. I was virtually speechless.

He continued, "We need the name and address of your church in order to verify the story (which was understandable) and to send the checks to your church for you."

I profusely thanked them and then returned to my knees and thanked God. I was transformed. My eyes were opened to what had just supernaturally occurred in my life. I had surrendered my pride. I had humbled myself before the Lord. I had surrendered all. By surrendering my pride, I allowed God to pour out His blessings for us. In other words, my pride had blocked God's blessings because I didn't want His help. I didn't truly trust His help. It wasn't until I let my pride fall down that I was then letting God do what was best for us. Pastor Joe used to say that so many times we sacrifice greatness on the altar of good. We settle for what we can achieve which is "good" and thereby lose what God can do which is "great". Just like a parent knows what is best for his child, so God knows what is best for us before we do. But He waits. He waits for us to draw closer to Him. Sometimes we do this easily, and sometimes we do this only once we have no other way out. In my case it was the hard way. I wouldn't have understood it if we hadn't been in this crisis. Either way, God waits for us.

After I realized all of this, I began to praise Him. I mean really praise Him. I never understood praise before. I only understood how to thank Him. I actually used to think that praising Him was sort of conceited on His part. Why would the creator of the universe create us just to say how great He is. That seemed cocky to me. I suddenly realized that the praise is a measure of our faith. It is for us not for Him. As we praise Him we are drawn into His glory. We are filled with an awesome closeness and enveloped with His love. I was able, for the first time in my life, to praise Him so genuinely. I felt so happy. It was a soul happiness.

My next epiphany was understanding what had held me back all these years from praising Him. It was pride. Pride inhibited my praise life. Pride blocked my vision. Pride focused me on myself and away from the Lord. Praise is gratitude. It is a trembling passion toward the One who shows you compassion and love. It is a profound appreciation as a result of realizing what God has done for you. Unless you can realize God's gifts to you, praise is not possible. It is also impossible to be double minded. It had to be one or the other. I was ready to release what I was holding onto to because I now understood the folly of pride and the glory of praise.

Chapter Four
Manna from Heaven—The Blessings

We received several gift certificates for supermarkets. We were being lifted up in prayer. We visited our old church and were handed a check from the deacons. A greeter that has always been so special to us was there. He suffered from arthritis in his hands. He went to shake Guy's hand which made Guy feel honored knowing the pain that this man suffered. But when their hands met, he slipped money into Guy's palm.

Cards came to us from people we had never met who were praying for us. Our church called us and told us that the check was in from Money Matters and that they would put it in the mail for us. A few days later, it came. I opened it up and gasped. It was for a significant amount. I had never expected such an outpouring. I thought at best, maybe a few people may help us out but never thought that there would be such an abundance. I cried. I cried some more. Folks that Guy and I didn't know and who didn't know us, cared for us enough to be so generous. They cared more for us than some people we knew. I was so flabbergasted. I called Guy at work and told him. He said he couldn't speak as he choked back tears of his own and hung up.

Some of our financial burdens were obvious. We had a mortgage, car payments, insurance, utilities and the like.

Additionally, we had child support to pay for Guy's daughter and a very expensive college as well. We prioritized this even above our mortgage bills. To minimize stress, Guy voluntarily set up payments through probation in order to avoid unpleasant phone calls and bickering. Therefore, we always made sure we cut the first check to the probation office. We depleted all of Guy's 401k funds, my 401k, his life insurance equity, and my sons' college funds in order to make sure child support was always paid. Along with our mortgage payments, the child support payments were always a source of concern and fear in the event that it could not be paid.

Our bible study was going strong. We met faithfully once a week and were still working on "Experiencing God". I would share everything that was happening to us on a weekly basis. One night before the study, one of the women , came up to me one night after our study and gave me a card with a check in it. She and her husband had felt so burdened for us and decided to help us. Her husband said he had received an extra paycheck this month and was distraught that Guy hadn't received any.

An old friend of mine, (who could write a book of her own) was a single mom raising two daughters and is on a tight budget, sent us a check.

In the spring of 2000, she came to know Jesus as her Lord and Savior. She has been on fire for him ever since. Her daughters also came to the Lord.

A few weeks ago, my friend found out that her youngest daughter was skipping school and getting involved in things that she shouldn't. She called me and asked if I would take her in for a while. She was hesitant in asking me because she knew the burdens we had. I explained to her that helping with her daughter would be a pleasure not a burden.

Her daughter stayed with us for about a week and then went to stay with her brother in another state. She started to have trouble there and we were on standby to drive down and bring her back. My heart was breaking. We loved her so much and I spent many hours on the phone with my friend trying to talk her through this, pray with her, and try to come up with solutions with no avail.

Pastor John stopped by to pick up his son who is a friend of DJ's. He had asked how things were going. This past New Year's Eve we had attended a party and he had been there. He had prayed with us when we didn't know exactly what to pray for. He asked God to give us manna from Heaven. That's it, I thought. That is exactly what we needed and didn't know how to ask. Maybe we were a little afraid to ask. So we updated him and told him how we were receiving exactly that which he had asked God to provide for us. We further told him of how first we had to lose our pride.

He surprised us by asking if Guy and I would speak at the youth group and give our testimony of how God has been working in our lives. I hadn't done public speaking since high school. I felt my heart start to palpitate and felt very nervous. My previous public speaking experience resulted in me feeling very frightened and lightheaded. But we promised to do it.

That Friday night we showed up at the youth group meeting. When it was my turn to speak, I explained that I was nervous and may pass out. But not to worry, I eventually would get back up again. A peel of laughter broke out and I was then put at ease. Guy and I explained what it was like on 9/11 but more importantly our walk of faith and all that we have been learning about God's faithfulness since then. We encouraged the teens to start trusting God now. We emphasized that tomorrow really isn't promised to us.

The 6 month anniversary was here. A video was on t.v. which had started out as a documentary of the NYFD. It turned out to be an eyewitness account of 9/11 from start to finish. We didn't watch any of the specials. We weren't ready. Guy had heard some things about the tape at work. When Guy came home he sat me down. He said, "I don't want you to say anything after I'm finished. Let me just share something with you without any comments."

"Okay."

"Do you remember when I told you that I had heard mini explosions in the mall of WTC 1?"

"Yes. You said you had nightmares of those sounds for months."

"Well, I now know what it was. It was the sound of the bodies hitting the ground."

I gasped. He started to cry. What do you say to something like that? We held each other without another word.

April rolled around and Guy was paid for the first time since December. Gratefulness was in my heart along with relief. We will now be able to get back on track, back to our lives. It'll take a little time to get our finances back in order but that was okay. It was at this point that I called my mother and told her what we had been going through. She scolded me for not telling her since she would have done whatever she could to help us. My mother had always been there for me through thick and thin. She was there for me as a teenager although I'm sure there were times she wished she was somewhere else! She was there as I went through a difficult marriage that ended only after four years. I was 25 years old at the time. She was there as I struggled as a single mom. My mom was the most consistent person in my life. That's exactly why I didn't tell you." Besides, she was 79 years old, had emphysema, two heart attacks, and quadruple bypass surgery. I didn't want to exacerbate her condition further. I knew it would be less traumatic to hear the events after the fact. I then called my father. He lived in New Hampshire. My parents had divorced when I was 12 years old and shortly afterwards my father had relocated to Washington, D.C. with his job. He worked for Radio Free Europe/Radio Liberty which would broadcast to countries behind the iron curtain. After a year, he relocated again. This time he went to Munich, Germany for a better position within Radio Free Europe. Although they were divorced, both of my parents had always shown love, concern, and a willingness to help the three of us. He had the same reaction but expressed gratitude that things were improving for us. He also told me to keep him informed going forward and if anything changes again to call him immediately. I was blessed to have the parents I have I thought.

Billy, who was here on 9/11 called. We eventually suggested that he and his family come out to church. They accepted the Lord after a while and started attending our church. One day, Billy called to say that his wife was gone. "Gone where?" I asked. His wife had been attending my bible study and hadn't mentioned any upcoming trips.

"No one knows. She's just gone." Guy told me.

An hour later, Guy's friend called to say that his wife had left a message that she went to see family and would be home Sunday. We thought that it was strange that she would just pick up and go without any forewarning. Sunday came and she returned. She explained that she thought she was going through menopause and just needed to take off for a little while. We were delighted that everything was okay and didn't give it any more thought.

Two more weeks passed and Guy received another check. We paid all our bills for the month now but were still not able to even meet the minimum due on our credit cards. Guy's car had recently broken down and needed $1500.00 worth of repairs as well as our water pump in the house! Goodbye paycheck!

I took DJ for a test drive prior to going for his license and discovered that the speed limit which usually never seemed like enough for me as a driver suddenly seemed way too fast. I explained to him that 55mph is the speed "limit" and it wasn't necessary to be right up against it. Afterwards he took his test and passed it with flying colors. Once we returned home, he asked to borrow the car.

"Why?"

"I just got my license. That's why."

"Isn't that enough for one day?" I asked.

"Come on Mom." So I conceded. I spent the day crying. I realized that going forward my life would never be the same. I would be in constant commune with God. I would be holding my breath from the time he left until the time he returned home. That's when I could exhale.

I ran into a friend at church who asked how things were going. Since my son's license was on my mind, I spewed all of my concerns. He just looked at me and said, "Don't you think that God could take better care of him than you can?" He was right. More humility. More pride was oozing out of me. Yes, oozing, like a bad infection.

When Tolyk came home from school, he told me that Tom had started up with him again spewing threats and making comments. Oh no, not again. This was the same chain of events as last time. I was afraid that it would also have the same outcome. There was no decision to make. I had to protect my son and not take any more chances. We took him out of the public school and put him in a small Christian school.

The next day, Tolyk's friend, stopped by unexpectantly. I wasn't expecting anyone since the kids were in school. He had the day off from work and had brought his mother over to meet me. She could only stay a few minutes. We exchanged pleasantries. She randomly told us about a second home that they own in Pennsylvania. They were selling it.

"You know sometimes we just do something and then ask God to bless it. That was our mistake. We couldn't afford to keep the house and didn't use it so we are forced to sell it."

"I'm sorry to hear about it," I said sincerely.

"Well, I just wanted to meet you. I have to run."

"Thanks for stopping by. It was nice meeting you." I thought hesitantly. It was odd. The spontaneous visit that was quite short-lived. What was the point of that? Then again I felt God hitting me over the head. "You do the same thing>" it seemed He was saying to me. "What?" just like a child I answered. You do it all on your own. Whether its decisions about schools, jobs, purchases, or even ministries, you do it on your own and then expect me to bless it. It's like marrying the wrong person and wanting your parent's blessing. WOW. I do that all the time. I need to come to Him first and with everything. Again, I was learning that everything belongs to Him, even my children. He was using His people to tell me such as the man at church and this woman popping over, were the mouthpieces for God. God's purpose wasn't to keep showing me I was wrong. He wanted me to have joy; the joy that comes from following in His ways and listening for Him. He will never lead me in the wrong direction if I would just rely on His wisdom instead of my own and walk in obedience.

Now it was May, again no paychecks. There was no indication of when the paychecks would come. There was the promise that as soon as the insurance settlement happened we would receive all of the back pay.

Billy called again. Again his wife had disappeared. This time she left a note that she went to the shore to think for a while. We spent some time over the weekend ministering to Billy. So many speculations were explored but were futile.

Unless she would explain what was going on in her heart, we would remain in the dark. At the end of the weekend, she returned. Our hearts had felt burdened for them. We again dismissed this as hormonal. But we knew that this would put a strain on their marriage. We prayed a lot for them. We prayed for my friend and her daughters. We added them to our perpetual prayer chains.

All of these issues were having a cumulative effect on us. Yet, when we worked with our friends' problems, it distracted us from our own. There was a sense of comfort in reaching out to help others

Pastor John called and asked if we would speak again at the church but this time for the business meeting. We agreed. After we spoke, the congregation prayed for us. Then Pastor John did something unexpected. He took a love offering for us. We fought the urge to decline. He told us that they would write out a check and we could pick it up tomorrow. Once again, people who didn't know us were caring for us. We were learning about Christian love. The love John spoke of when he said, John 13:35

"By this everyone will know that you are my disciples, if you love one another."

I used to think we were generous people when we had money. We gave to the church, we gave to ministries, we gave to the people in our lives that we knew and loved. But we never gave to the extent that we were now receiving. We didn't usually give money to people whom we didn't know or if we did, it was a minimal amount. We thanked Jesus for people who were more giving than we were. We again stood humbled before Him. But we were learning what an obedient Christian does.

Chapter Five
In the Valley

Finally Pastor Joe approached us and said the deacons were against the computer ministry because of a lack of space in the building. Wow, no room at the inn, huh. We were quite disillusioned. We felt so strongly about this ministry. We had seen the positive results from our previous church. It's a great outreach program and the door was just slammed in our faces.

Guy remembered that our local mall had a mall ministry which we had attended for a prayer vigil on September 14, 2001. He called the director and discussed the computer ministry with her. After listening to all the details, she said, I'm very excited about this class and feel it would be an excellent outreach program.

Guy asked, "But first you have to ask the board right?"

"No. How soon do you want to start?"

"I can't believe it. That's it? You want this ministry just like that?"

"Yes. What do you need us to do to get this started?"

"Well I have all the computers ready, I would just need tables to set them up. We will need to advertise the classes, print out some brochures and pick a start date."

"We'll do all the advertising and get all the names and numbers into a database. Could you write up the brochure?"

"Sure. This is great. We'll set up a date and get started. How about June 13th?"

"That's fine."

"Thank you so much. Bye."

Now it was May and again no paychecks. There was no indication of when the paychecks would come. Well, I'm just going to keep trusting God. He has brought us this far and I knew that Jesus said, "I will never leave you or forsake you." Joshua 1:5. Here the operative words are He will never "Leave" nor "forsake". He is always by our sides. If we were only able to see Him walking next to us, we would never be fearful again. To "see" Him walking next to us doesn't necessarily mean with eyesight. Rather it is with insight.

We received a message on the answering machine which was a law firm and wanted Guy to call back immediately. Since Guy was at work, I called. The man was an ornery person who demanded that I prove who I am. Shaken by the fact that I was dealing with a law firm, I allowed this man to cross examine me.

"What is your full legal name?"

I told him.

"What is your mailing address?" Again I furnished the information.

"What is your husband's social security number?"

It was apparent to me at this point to stop answering these questions. Something just didn't seem right.

"Sir, I have answered all of your questions, now I would like to know who you are and what this is pertaining to?"

"I'll ask the questions." He bellowed into the phone. "Don't you understand that this is a very serious legal matter?! You better just make sure that your husband calls me."

The phone went dead. I called Guy at work and gave him the number. He also did not receive any answers. This man merely laughed whenever Guy asked what this was in regard to and said 'I'll see you in court.' It is interesting how a person who Is feeling vulnerable can be subjected so easily to answering questions and submitting to someone else who is acting authoritatively. There is a sense of lowness and unworthiness and therefore, feel that we owe others whatever they may ask of us.

We had no idea what this was but we were rattled. The next day a letter came in the mail. The return address had the name of the law firm that had contacted us yesterday. It was a letter threatening to sue us for the money we owed on the credit card. The all familiar question came up once again. "What were we going to do?" We had no money for credit card bills. It's difficult for me to say but with the money we had received we had to take care of mortgage, child support, etc. and the credit card bills were at the bottom of the list of priorities. We discussed this issue for a while. We had exhausted all possibilities. There was no way out. We were going to be sued by this credit card company. We still had no way to pay let alone catch up. We would have to file for bankruptcy. There was a significant air of shame in this for both of us. Although this was not our fault, there was still a sense of guilt. Even though we had been able to pay monthly pre-9/11, thoughts came to me that had we just not racked up the charges before we would not be in this situation. Debt consolidation was out because there is a monthly amount that has to be steady and one has to be able to commit to, which we could not do. We cannot always plan for the future but we soon learned that anything can happen. We need to avoid financing as much as possible and pay things with cash. We now had no choice because with bankruptcy, not only are your debts eliminated but so is your credit rating and financial standing.

Regret filled me for even using credit cards. Why do we always try to live beyond our means? Sometimes an emergency does arise and the cards come in handy, but primarily we used them casually. We had to call the lawyer and start the process. It's a very tedious process. All tax returns, mortgage statements, lists of belongings, and much more need to be provided. My fax machine was always tied up with correspondence to and from the attorney. I felt very low. I wondered if God would turn his face away from us now.

As the paper trail continued, we needed to reaffirm certain loans which included the mortgage company and car bills. The car finance company sent the appropriate paperwork and we filled out all the necessary information. Our attorney then instructed us that the mortgage company would do the same.

June was upon us now. The weather was beautiful; the air was crisp and clean. The gardening had been done, the goats had yielded several kids, and the promise of summer was in the air. The sound of baby chicks peeping was like a symphony. This time of the year always seemed so inspiring and rejuvenating.

On June 13th we started computer classes. We had 11 students and a waiting list of 84 people. We were so amazed at the response. There clearly was a need for this ministry. It was a blessing to be a part of it. The first class went well and we were really excited. The course was an eight week course and we were looking forward to what God would do with it. He already showed us why He closed the door at our church. He had different plans for our ministry than we did. He opened the door at the mall ministry and we are about to reach tons of people. Once again, we received a reminder that we needed to trust Him more and lean not on our understanding. Our understanding had led to our disappointment and our lack of trust until we had hindsight.

The next day my Dad called from New Hampshire. After chatting pleasantly for a while (I didn't tell him what occurred since April), he told me he needs to tell me something. He had been diagnosed with lung cancer. I was in shock. He had quit smoking over a year ago. We talked about it for a while and I tried to give him some hope. I hung up the phone and cried. When Guy came home from work I told him about Dad. He said to call him back and let him know that he would be coming up tonight to get him and bring him down for the weekend. We needed to have a family meeting to decide what the best treatments would be.

It was a 7 hour trip to New Hampshire. Guy did a marathon trip by picking up my Dad and driving straight home. They arrived early Saturday morning. Once here, my Dad told me that the cancer had spread to his liver, and bones, another shock. What did this mean? What was the prognosis? We begged my Dad to move down here. He said he would like to but had to go through many personal belongings. He was also working on an autobiography about his experiences in a communist country and fighting in World War II. He said it would take time. Perhaps next Spring. He also begged me not to worry.

He said, "You have enough things to worry about. Don't worry about me honey. I'm prepared for whatever happens. Please don't worry."

I fought back the tears. I couldn't believe his composure. We talked a lot that weekend. My brothers had come down to see him also. I gave them some time to talk with him one on one. It was time again to draw on strength and character. My father was the one showing me how to do it.

On Wednesday Guy drove my Dad back to New Hampshire. We exchanged tearful goodbyes and he promised to keep me updated on his condition. He would begin chemotherapy the following week.

Billy came by. His wife was gone again. This time there were no messages and some of her belongings were missing.

We spent hours discussing the possibilities. When he returned home, she was there. She told him that she was moving out. She indicated that this was just temporarily until she gets her thoughts together. It was time to be concerned. This wasn't a hormonal thing anymore. We extended an invitation to Billy to spend time with us whenever he needed it. Guy and I knew we had to guide him in a Christian walk as he went through such a difficult time. We had each gone through a difficult divorce in the past and knew what was involved. We knew God was using our trials to be able to minister to Billy. God, will use your experiences to help others as they walk through the fire. There was an abundant amount of love in our hearts despite our circumstances and we wanted to be of help.

Guy started sending out his resume just to be on the safe side. It was an attempt to see what was out there and to line up his ducks if the need arose. He had sent out over a hundred resumes. We anticipated the bombardment of recruiters with dread.

One week went by and then the next. No one had called. He was always being seduced by one headhunter or another but now there was silence. He called some old contacts that were always trying to lure him away. Sorry, they said, we have a hiring freeze. But you'll be the first one we call. He had sent out over one hundred resumes and had no response.

At the end of June, we attended a seminar for couples sponsored by Family Life. It was exclusive for firemen and policemen that had worked at the World Trade Center disaster. When Guy called them and said he was a survivor they told by all means we should come. So we did. I was hedging. I didn't need a support group. My impression was a group of very depressed people sharing the horrors they experienced. Guy tried to coax me and I eventually yielded. When we got there, I was genuinely surprised. It was geared more to keeping couples growing together even during hard times. We spoke with a few of the coordinators of the seminar and Guy promised to email his testimony to them.

My mother was losing weight unintentionally. After a visit with her internist, he sent her for an ultra sound on her kidneys. After a week's waiting period, the report came back negative. But we still didn't know why she was losing so much wait. After another visit to her internist, he sent her for an ultra sound of her liver and gall bladder. When the report came in it showed that she had gallstones although she didn't seem to have any sensitivity or other symptoms, she would eventually need surgery.

I was due for my annual ob/gyn exam. They did the routine tests and told me if I didn't hear from them in 10 days to call. Seven days later they called and left a message with my son late in the afternoon on a Friday. By the time I got the message, the office was closed. A terrible feeling of foreboding enveloped me. They never call. I always have had to call after ten days to find out that everything was normal. They must be calling to tell me bad news.

On Monday, I was able to get through to the office. After being on hold for what seemed an eternity, the nurse came on and said that my test had come back abnormal.

They put me on medication. She said after you finish your medication, wait two weeks and then come back to repeat the test. I finished the medication, waited two weeks, and then waited another two weeks for an available appointment.

The following week my brother Tony had to go for a routine stress test. Afterwards he called me fearfully. While on the treadmill, his heart had a sudden reaction. He felt a sharp pain. The doctor took him off and gave him nitroglycerin. The doctor wanted him immediately to go for an echocardiogram. After the electrocardiogram They were now sending him for a catharization. There were waivers to sign and warnings that the procedure could result in a stroke, heart attack, and even death. I contacted all the prayer chains that I could think of. It seemed we were perpetually on the prayer lists.

It was time for me to retake my test. This time it came back abnormal again. The next step would be a biopsy through a procedure called a colposcopy. All I understood was that something was abnormal.

Meanwhile, Tony's catherization indicated that he needed bypass surgery. After speaking to him on the phone, I sat down on our back porch and cried again. What was happening to our family? The pressure didn't seem to let up, not even a little. No sooner did one situation finish than another began. How much stress can one bear?

Tony's bypass was a success. After he gets released from the hospital he would have to begin rehabilitation exercises but his prognosis was positive. I stayed with his wife on the day of the catherization and the day of the bypass.

The day of the colposcopy arrived. I hated going to ob/gyn anyway but today I dreaded it more. The procedure is quite "up close and personal" and it hurts! My mistake was in going alone. My lower extremities trembled as I drove home. I managed but it would have been more comfortable if I didn't have to drive. It would be another two weeks before the results came in.

I called after the waiting period and was told that my chart was in the other office in a nearby town. I called the other office. They told me they couldn't find my chart and would get back to me. When they didn't call back, I called. Eventually they found my file. The nurse hesitated and then said, "according to the results, everything seems to be fine." Relief washed over me. It's amazing to think that I didn't realize how much stress I was experiencing over this until I received my results. It was as if I was emotionally holding my breath and now could breathe again.

A neighbor of my father's called. He was in the hospital. The diagnosis was dehydration. I called the hospital. My Dad informed me that he was feeling better now that they were rehydrating him. However, he needed a blood transfusion. He was tired and weak and couldn't stay on the phone. We were back on the prayer lists and back on my knees.

At the end of July, Guy again received a paycheck. Again in the beginning of August he received another. It seemed that we were getting back on track. However, we still were in a very deep home and would take more than this to dig our way out of financial ruin.

It was time to finalize our bankruptcy. At the courthouse, we were stunned by the amount of people waiting to be free of their debts. Our application was reviewed but there was information missing. They postponed our hearing for two weeks.

Two weeks later, we met in the trustee's office. He reviewed our case and said he would recommend dismissal of our debts. I felt ashamed yet at the same time felt a tremendous amount of relief. This of course reduced our liability quite a bit. It made it less burdensome to try and find money to pay our bills.

After another two weeks, we received a court motion in the mail! It was a motion to "vacate to stay" in order to proceed with foreclosure. Foreclosure??? Our house had never been up for foreclosure. I didn't understand what any of this meant. Vacate to stay seemed like a contradiction of terms. I was in a panic. The possibility of losing our home was my worst nightmare. We didn't even have money nor a good credit standing to start over with another house or apartment.

I put this in God's hands. He must have very large hands because I was starting to put a lot in them on faith. I called the lawyer. He told me not to worry (famous last words). It was merely a formality. Because of the bankruptcy, our creditors were not allowed to contact us and that they were petitioning to lift the restriction. I asked him why it referred to a foreclosure. Although he had never come across that before, he was certain it was merely because it was a standard form that they used.

Our next step was to reaffirm the loan. What? It turned out that we needed to prepare the reaffirmation agreement and send it to them. Not the other way around. This little detail had not been handled. We could lose our home because of a legal oversight. Our attorney contacted the attorney for our mortgage company. He explained the circumstances and we filed the reaffirmation agreement. After several treacherous weeks of waiting, and many panic attacks, the motion was lifted. We then had to pay for our mortgage company's legal fees. But the matter finally was put to rest.

Chapter Six
Delighting in Trials

The one year anniversary was drawing near. Our home church had asked Guy to give his testimony at their 9/11 Remembrance. Also he was approached to speak at an Ecumenical service locally on 9/11. Evangelism Today (a syndicated Christian Radio Program) asked for an interview at their studios.

An e-mail came from a gentleman by the name of Craig Furhman formerly of Campus Crusades for Christ. He had received Guy's testimony from when Guy had e-mailed his testimony to the people at FamilyLife back in July. Craig was from Weare, NH. His church was sponsoring a town wide Remembrance on September 15 with music, food, and speakers. He wanted Guy and I to be the main speakers. It was an opportunity to share our experience as well as our faith since it would be primarily a secular crowd. They expected approximately 2000 people in attendance.

Neither of us had ever spoken before a crowd of this magnitude. Could we handle this, I wondered. This was definitely bigger than us. This was (as Henry Blackwell would call it) a God-sized assignment. Putting our reservations aside, we realized that if God wanted us to do it, He would see us through it. We committed to Craig and finalized the details. He and his wife graciously invited us to stay with them at their lake house for the weekend.

The September 8th presentation at our home church went well. The Salvation Army played patriotic songs followed by David Verkler from Dedicated Evangelism who spoke. The church, courtesy of CBN News, had spliced the interview with Guy together with the clips of 9/11 and played the video. It was a moving experience. Guy finished the program with a recap of the events and the blessings and lessons he has received thus far.

The next morning, I was informed that my father was back in the hospital. Again he was admitted for dehydration. On Tuesday, he was receiving a blood transfusion since his red blood cells had dropped drastically and his white blood count was quite high.

We left early in the morning on September 12th for New Hampshire with our first stop at the hospital in Dover, NH. After seven hours we arrived. We dropped the boys off at the hotel and ran up to the hospital. I wasn't prepared for what I saw next. My father had no hair, looked very pale, and was quite emaciated. He was a mere 139 pounds and stood at 5'9.

He greeted us with a huge smile and urged us to go and rest at the hotel and to come back in the morning. That was his way. I had brought him two Christian books. I knew that my father believed in God, the resurrection, and prayed daily yet, I wasn't sure if he really made Jesus Lord of his life. Even if he didn't read the books, having them on the table may invite a nurse or nurse's aid who are believers to strike up a conversation with him.

We went back to the hotel. We gathered up the boys and returned to the hospital for a brief moment. He told us that the transfusion had been successful and that he was starting to feel much better. His doctor would be doing his rounds in the morning and would give me more details. We then grabbed a quick meal and went back to the hotel.

I tossed and turned all night. It's hard to sleep in a strange bed besides the image of my Dad laying there so thin haunted my sleep. This image haunted me even in my sleep.

In the morning we headed back to my father. I met his doctor. Although he was a general practitioner and not his oncologist, he was treating my father's dehydration and had ordered the transfusion. After being updated and told that my father was being released tomorrow, we arranged to have meals on wheels set up for him. After a tearful goodbye, we set out for Weare which was about an hour away from Dover.

The Furhmans greeted us warmly as we arrived. They had a beautiful home on a manmade lake. The scenery was beautiful. Majestic trees surrounded the lake giving one a sense of privacy. They had a small speed boat and we hopped in for a tour around the lake. Their church was having a pot luck supper that evening in our honor. We were to give them a synopsis of our speech and then open for questions. The food was scrumptious and the people were delightful. It was a great night of fellowshipping and of course, good food.

Saturday morning came quickly and we took a short drive around the area. The mountains were quite charming. We geared up for the evening remembrance which would begin at 6:00.

The hour arrived before we knew it and we headed out to the grounds. Weare, NH has approximately a population of 7,000 people.

The junior and senior high school band played an array of patriotic songs which always chokes me up. A few policeman and fireman stood up and were honored. I can't recall what was said because I was quite nervous. Guy & I would give our account verbally, as is in Chapter one of this book. I prayed and prayed for God to just let the Holy Spirit guide me and take away my nervousness. Before I was done praying, I heard our names being called. The sun had gone down and a flood light blinded me as I stepped up on the stage. Looking back, it probably made it easier for me not being able to actually see the audience. I was told that there were about 1200 in attendance.

Guy concluded our speech with a candid expression of his faith not knowing how the crowd would respond to this yet, he was not concerned. He boldly spoke of his Lord and Savior and gave proof of His existence in our lives. We were hopeful that even one person would be touched and maybe seek God. When he was done, the crowd stood up and gave him a standing ovation bringing tears to my eyes. We weren't celebrities, we weren't entertainers, we were merely eyewitnesses to God's grace. When God gives you a testimony, you need to share it. Not for self-edification but to glorify Him and reach those that He puts in your path.

A few people in the crowd came up to speak to us. Two policemen shook our hands and said, "God bless you. Thank you for your testimony." It was music to our ears. We also asked for God's blessings upon them. The Pastor of the sponsoring church stayed nearby in case someone wanted to know more about Jesus.

The next day we thanked our host and hostess. They gave us an unexpected offering. Every time was just as hard as the first but God has humbled us enough to realize we accept His blessings with a grateful heart.

On Sunday we went to my Father's apartment. I was aghast when I saw the inside. Due to his illness, he hadn't been able to clean other than a quick scrub down of the bathroom sink and toilet. Dust was everywhere. So were taped up boxes. Dirt was heavy on the floor. There weren't any dishes in the sink because he wasn't eating much. I needed to clean it. I just couldn't stand seeing the condition in which he lived with no one to help him. After visiting for an hour or two, I started cleaning. He was concerned about our long drive home and insisted that I stop and leave before it gets too dark. I reluctantly listened. I was very sorry to leave him in these conditions. I had a hard time leaving him period. We tried to convince him to move in with us. He said that maybe in the spring. He still had a lot of boxes and papers to go through in order to liquidate some things he has kept for years. We told him that we would help him but he still declined. Shortly afterwards, we left for home.

The following week I called his oncologist. We discussed my Dad's condition in great detail. I saved the real question for last. This was the question that I didn't really want to hear the answer. I swallowed hard and asked, "I know you can't give me an exact time, but how much time do you think my father has left?"

"It's hard for me to say. Each patient's condition is different."

"Are we talking about a year or more."

"Oh no. It's more a matter of months."

"Thank you doctor. I appreciate you taking out the time to talk with me."

"I'm sorry. This shouldn't happen to anyone. Especially someone as nice as your father."

"Thank you." I hung up the phone shakily. My heart felt like it was being ripped apart. Tolyk survived Lyme Disease, Guy survived the attack on the World Trade Center. In this case, my father wasn't going to survive. Cancer had threatened my father before. In 1990, he had Prostrate Cancer and had surgery to remove it, along with radiation treatments. A few years later, he was diagnosed with T-Cell Lymphoma and received treatments for that. Now, in 2002, he had Lung Cancer. Parents are there from the very beginning of one's life. Although we know that we are hopefully to outlive them, it's hard to imagine a life without them. Their presence was constant. I didn't see myself as one of those folks who have lost a parent. Not me. I always had my parents. It occurred to me that my father may not know his prognosis. I was embarking on the worst thing I have ever had to do. I had to call him and tell him that he would die. How? How do I say it without falling apart? How do I say it casually? This would be the hardest conversation I have ever had with anyone. How do you tell your father he is dying soon. Do I use a clinical tone especially over the phone? Do I show my fear? Do I let myself start crying in front of him? I prayed and then I dialed his number.

"Daddy?"

"Hi honey! How are you?"

"I'm okay. Daddy, I just spoke with your doctor."

"Oh, and?"

"He explained your condition to me in great detail. I asked him for a prognosis. I took a deep breath. "Daddy, he said it's a matter of months. Daddy, I'm so so sorry."

"Well, my time has come. It's okay honey. Don't be sad. It's okay. Please don't worry." He paused and said, "Well, what do you think? Should I still come to live with you?"

"Of course. We should make it soon. How about October 15?"

"Oh that's too soon. I have a lot to arrange."

"Dad, we have to do this quickly. We'll come up and help you."

"Okay honey dear. But please don't worry."

"I love you."

"I love you too."

I went out and sat on the stairs of our deck. Through the window I could hear DJ practicing piano. It blended into the background until I suddenly realized the name of the piece he was playing. "My Heart will go on" from the movie "Titanic". The song took on a personal meaning for me. I couldn't hold back the tears. Not my father I thought. This doesn't happen to our family. I have always had my parents. Other people are parentless. Everything that was happening to us happens to "other people". I pictured my father sitting alone in his small, dark apartment having to deal with the realization that not only is his life ending but it is ending soon. I calmed myself down knowing I still had to call the rest of the family.

I quickly called my brothers while I still had my composure. They took it pretty hard and I could not hold back when I told them. We discussed the arrangements to bring him here. The conversations were short. Each one of us wanted to handle this in our own way alone. The grieving had already begun. That's the heart-wrenching part to a terminal illness. The mourning happens while the person is alive. It feels like a betrayal. I felt guilty for grieving. I almost felt like I was pushing him into the grave by feeling this way. More irrational emotions ran rapid.

A local Christian radio station was running a share-a-thon all week. We didn't have money to donate, so instead, Guy volunteered to answer the phones for two hours each day for that week. At the end of the week, he had felt more productive at the radio station for two hours a day, than at work for eight hours.

On October 4, I received a phone call that yet again my Dad was hospitalized for dehydration. It was at this time that we decided to bring him home with us immediately. He couldn't keep dehydrating. He lived alone and wasn't eating or drinking properly. This was sure to shorten his already shortened life. On October 6th, Guy and my brother Tony were on their way to New Hampshire to pack up the apartment and abduct my father. There was so much to arrange. I contacted his doctors to arrange an early discharge. I had to order all of his medical records to be ready to go home with him on October 8th. I made an appointment here with a general practitioner who then referred me to a radiologist and an on radiation oncologist. My brother was going to handle cancelling the electricity, propane gas, telephone, cable, mail and banks.

Tolyk volunteered to surrender his room for my Dad. We spent the day rearranging the family room, which was to be Tolyk's new room, and setting up my father's room. Sunday my sister-in-law came over to help me with shopping and sanitizing the house. By Monday, we were ready. They rolled in around 9:00p.m. My Dad looked worse than he did last month. He was vomiting. He was very weak. He went to bed immediately.

The next day we had our first appointment. After the visit the doctor recommended setting him up on hospice to give these last months of his life some dignity. By Wednesday, all of his hospital equipment arrived. Hospice called and made an appointment for Thursday. I was amazed and grateful for the efficient and expeditious manner in which everything had been arranged.

The next morning, hospice had sent a counselor to address any of our concerns and questions. She asked if I wanted a home health aid. I said no. For now, I could handle taking care of my father. I didn't want him to feel dependent on too many people. Shortly after the counselor came the nurse also came. She introduced herself, gave me some more information and set up a weekly appointment.

A few days later we met with the radiologist who set up appointments for palliative radiation for the bone pain. This is only to relieve some of the pain and not a cure. It's for 10 sessions everyday except on weekends and lasts about 15 minutes after the initial appointment which is about 45 minutes. He had to be taken off of hospice while going through the treatments and then would be put back on due to Medicare restrictions.

The next day we went for the first appointment which is just the evaluation. While waiting, I took note of some of the other people waiting for their sessions. A few elderly gentlemen sat in wait and a young woman sat with her mother. I wondered what they were feeling and thinking. The young woman was called next. I was surprised. I thought she too had brought her mother. Now it seemed that she was suffering with cancer. I listened as the staff laughed and joked with one another, planned their lunch menus and carried on casually. There was such a disparity in the room. There were those who seemingly had normal lives and those who didn't. My father's session was soon over and we went home.

In the morning we had to see the oncologist prior to the radiation therapy. He carried on a conversation with my father. He mentioned that he has a sister who also lives in New Hampshire. We asked him in which town and he said, "Oh it's a little town called 'Weare'. "My husband and I just did a 9/11 remembrance up there. If she didn't attend the event she surely will be receiving my husband's testimony in the mail." I didn't know what the connection was but I'm sure God did.

After he evaluated my father's case history, he stated that it was important to keep the remainder of his life with dignity and grace. By trying to save his life we would shorten it even more. There was nothing left to do. He also said it would probably be a matter of months.

My father responded with, "There's a German song that says, "All things come to an end. Now my life will do the same. Thank you doctor." He stood with dignity, grace, and a smile on his face. I, on the other hand, again had to choke back the tears.

We went downstairs for the treatment. Since my dad received 3 radiation treatments in NH prior to coming to NJ, we only had to do 7 sessions. This was the first of the 7 sessions.

Chapter Seven
Tomorrow May Not Come

At radiation, I again noticed the young lady with her mother. I said a polite hello and nothing more. I used the time to prepare my bible study lessons. By the third session, my father's back pain seemed to actually become increasingly worse. As I waited for him, the young lady came in with her mother. Again I gave a polite hello as I looked up from my book. I felt an urging to strike up a conversation. I thought, 'I don't want to'. I wasn't in the mood to socialize today. I went back to my book. Again, an urging to converse. I knew it was God. He was pushing me out of my comfort zone. Again, I resisted. Sadly, I often argue with God when I don't want to do something that he wants me to do out of my "zone". 'Fine, I thought.

"How are you doing today?"

"I'm tired but doing better."

"I'm glad to hear it. How many sessions do you have left?"

"This time, eight."

"What do you mean."

"Well, I'm 23 years old. When I was 21, they found a spot on my lung that went down to the bone. They said I probably had it since my teens. They were able to eliminate it with chemotherapy and radiation. A short time ago, I was having headaches and blurred vision. I went to the eye doctor. It wasn't my eyes. I then went for a cat scan and they found 3 inoperable tumors. They are trying the radiation but have told me that I probably have a few weeks to live. I have three little ones at home and I'm not giving up."I was speechless for a moment. Then more urging came. It was like my mouth opened and words just came out.

"You need to return to the Lord, you know."

"Yes, I know. The Pastor had come from my mother's church to see me and the church is praying for me."

"That is wonderful. But you still have to make a decision to let Jesus be the Lord of your life and put your trust in Him no matter what happens."

"Yeah, I know."

Just then my father was wheeled back in to me and it was time to go.

"I'll pray for you. See you tomorrow." I couldn't believe the exchange that just went on. I have never been that bold but it seemed so natural as we spoke. It seemed to be such a necessary conversation. I shared her story with my father and he said that's why he isn't sorry about his situation. After all, he said, "I've lived a long life. It's such a shame when this happens to someone so young."

That evening, a woman from my bible study and I were talking on the phone. I shared the event of the day with her. She suggested I get Barbara Johnson's book, "Put a geranium in my cranium." She said it talks about faith, cancer, and adds humor.

I ran to the Christian bookstore and purchased the book. I waited for two days before giving her the book. I told the woman I had a present for her. She told me that she hasn't read anything but Dr. Seuss since she had children. I encouraged her to start reading this book.

At the next session, I again saw the woman. She said, "I started reading the book last night and I am almost done with it."

"That's great. I hope you could glean some comfort and humor from it. More importantly I hope it brings you closer to God."

She thanked me. I told her we were done with our treatments tomorrow. The following day, we said goodbye and I promised to pray for her.

My Dad's back pain got worse. His medicines were increased. So did his vomiting. He ate very small meals. His meals usually consisted of a piece of buttered toast and tea for breakfast, soup, toast, juice, and jell-O for lunch, and a small portion of whatever we are having for dinner.

The following week his pain was much better. The doctor told us that the pain would increase and then about one to two weeks after radiation he will feel a marked improvement. Dad was so happy to be relieved of the pain.

I made a Thanksgiving dinner at the beginning of November. I didn't want him to have to wait for Thanksgiving Day. He was so delighted with the food that he snuck into the kitchen and helped himself to seconds. I was thrilled. I deluded myself to think this was a sign that he was doing better.

Guy offered to read the bible with my father as a historic document. This appealed to him since he was a political scientist and had casually read the bible in his youth. Every night Guy read to him from the book of John. It was Thursday night and Guy was at the computer class. Normally he is home by 7:30. As I cooked dinner I heard what I thought was a moan from my father. I peeked my head into the living room and heard him say, "Guy. Guy. Well, I guess we're not going to read tonight." I told him Guy would be home around 9:30 because he was teaching tonight.

"Oh alright. He'll probably be too tired to read."

"We'll see Dad."

It was so endearing to know that he was enjoying the bible readings so much. I was praying fervently that it was taking a hold of his heart. I knew that my father believed in God, knew much of the bible, believed in the resurrection and the trinity, but I needed for my sake, to know that he believed that Jesus was his Savior and Lord. I needed to hear the words. My Dad came from a generation that believed that religion was a private matter so I wasn't sure if Jesus was definitely in his heart or just in his mind.

When Guy came home at 9:30 he said, "I'm sure you're tired so we'll just read tomorrow."

"No. Let's read now."

"Oh yeah", my father said with enthusiasm and pushed himself up into a sitting position.

The medication would take its toll on my Dad. Due to the tumor also being on his liver, the medication wasn't being properly filtered and would affect his entire system rendering him nauseous, weak, and slightly disorientated. He would suddenly forget how to use the remote control for the television and lose track of the days. His legs would get very weak and need assistance to walk from room to room. He would eat three meals a day but very small portions. He would sleep quite a bit and of course, forget what each of his pills were for. Although, with the amounts of pills he had to take this was understandable. He had a long lasting pill for pain, a breakthrough pill for pain, a pill for coughing, a pill for nausea, a pill for acid inhibition, and medicine for constipation, all of which he had to take several times a day. I had set up a chart because it's easy to forget when the next doses were due. All in all the medications did keep him comfortable. Yet, he was losing a lot of weight and was growing progressively weak.

He started to lose interest in the news (which used to be his life-line) but he did enjoy watching all the old sitcoms. Sometimes we would enjoy them and laugh, sometimes he would fall asleep to them. In either case, he wanted things light and airy.

He would remember that he had to pay his bills and would ask for them. I would tell him not to worry about it because Tony was taking care of all of that. He accepted this. That came as a surprise to me. It. wasn't like him. He was the type of person that would then remind us to make sure we didn't overlook something...ask a lot of questions about how Tony is managing all of this, if his bills were now forwarded here or to Tony's etc. Instead, he just said okay. It was as if this was another part of his life that was over and he was accepting it and adjusting to it.

I would spend hours in the garage going through his boxes. I was checking for things that he needed and things that I needed to go through. I did this now because I didn't know if I could handle it after he was gone. I came across his phone book and extra glasses which made him very happy to have. He didn't use his phone book because he was too tired. But he was happy that he had his usual belongings. I came across all the cards we had ever sent to him. I came across phone bills from 1962! He had taken such great pains to keep so many things. Some were so irrelevant and some were so precious.

I would keep my brothers updated with progress reports. I would talk with my mother. She would comfort me and just fill air time with updates on the news and anything else that came to mind.

Our church signed us up for meals. Every week, our friends from church, Donna and Mark, would drop off 4 or 5 dinners for the week made by various people in the church. My Dad always looked forward to their visit and the treats that they would bring. It was such a relief not to have to stay on top of extra cooking. I could feed Guy and the boys with these and then tend to my Dad.

Chapter Eight
Death is Precious to the Lord

It was all unreal. I was going through the motions. I was playing nurse and acting clinically yet at times I wanted just to be Daddy's little girl, crawl up on his lap and have him tell me, everything would be okay. Tell me this would pass. Somehow, Daddy would make this alright and everything, everything, would be just as it used to be. How I longed for that. At times, he did. He would look at me and say, "Sweetheart, you are such a great daughter. I know this is so hard for you. I'm sorry you have to go through this. It's okay, I'm not scared, I'm happy. I'm really happy to be here. I'm ready to face what's ahead."

"Daddy, I'll be here for you all the way." was all I could muster to say.

His eating habits had slowed down. He didn't desire lunch just a jell-O or fruit cup. One morning I came into his room and he said, "I'm having trouble breathing. Open a window." (It was November at this point and cold outside)

"Dad, I don't want you to be in a draft, you could catch a cold."

"Well, it doesn't matter, if I can't breathe." he said calmly.

"Oh, you're right." and I opened the window. I was so focused on the minors I had overlooked the majors. Thankfully he was able to still be practical! Sometimes, as caregivers, we get stuck on the daily routines and the obvious concerns such as avoid any contact with germs and colds because he is more vulnerable now, that we miss some of the common sense ones such as opening the window to help him breathe. However, in my defense, I knew that he could breathe, because after all, he was able to tell me that he couldn't breathe. It was more of a sensation that people with pulmonary issues feel. I was told by a friend of mine who was a nurse, that often, it helps just to set up a fan next to their bed or chair because the air blowing directly on their face seems to help them feel that they can breathe better. So a new fan it is!

I had picked up all sorts of small comforts for him. Ensure to drink, baby wipes, Clorox wipes to clean the bathroom, microwavable bath cloths that are pre-moistened. I walked into his bathroom to ritually clean and noticed that the baby wipes were still untouched. However, the Clorox wipes were almost gone! a cold sweat came over me. Oh no, he's using the wrong wipes! I panicked.

"Dad are these the wipes you've been using?"

"I guess so."

"Dad, these are Clorox wipes. They have bleach in them."

"So what? It's not bothering me."

I realized I was stressing for nothing. Really what was the big deal as long as he didn't feel any irritation. It was more upsetting to him to remember which container is for what than just using whichever one was handy. However, I did remove the Clorox ones and relocated them to the hall closet to avoid a future mix-up.

In the late evening on November 3 my Dad called for me. He said, "Something just isn't right. Perhaps I should go to the hospital."

"Dad, can you be more specific? They won't take you just based on 'something just isn't right.'

"I can't explain it. It's just a general feeling of malaise."

"I'll call hospice."

I left a message for the on-call nurse who called me back within minutes. She advised me to give him a little anti-anxiety medicine. "But he's not really anxious," I said. That's okay it may help to relax him and this general feeling of malaise may pass.

I told him the nurse wanted me to give him a new medicine. He said good just being in touch with a medical person made him feel content. After administering the Lorazepam, he quieted down and went to sleep. The next morning he was out cold. I called our regular hospice nurse and my brother. They both arrived around the same time.

She sat us down and explained to us that he is in the end stage. We asked if we should take him to the hospital and she said it was our choice however, it will just mean that he will be full of tubes and in more discomfort than being home with his family in peace. She also said don't try to pump him with liquids or food unless he requests them. It may actually make him more uncomfortable. She gave us a report about dehydration in cancer patients in the end stage. She also asked me if at this time I would like to have a home health aid come to wash and shave him and change the linens. I gave in and said yes knowing that now he would prefer for me not to do it out of a sense of pride and I wanted to respect his privacy.

That afternoon the home health aid arrived, her name was Sophie. She was a young pretty woman from Poland who was studying to be a nurse and working for Samaritan Hospice while she went to school. This is perfect I thought. He knows how to speak Polish, he has a lot in common with her and when he recovers from this bout he will enjoy her company. Then I remembered what the nurse had told us about this being the end stage and most likely he will not recover.

I liked Sophie immediately. She was professional and compassionate. She went about her business talking to my father although there were no signs that he heard her. We could roll him over or ask him to sit up but he was clearly out of it and wouldn't verbally respond.

The next morning he was still in the same state. I thought, "What have I done. I knocked him out with this medication." I spoke to Sophie and she said that the Lorazepam was quite mild and wouldn't have an effect on her or me. But because his liver isn't functioning properly it will hit him harder than a healthy person.

The following day, I heard his bell ringing. I ran into his room to find him sitting up smiling and he said, "I'm hungry." I was overjoyed. He had rebounded and we had him back with us. I immediately got his breakfast and explained what had taken place the last few days. He had no recall and didn't even realize that three days had gone by. I told him about the home health aid and he was looking forward to meeting her. Today is also his birthday. He turned 83.

I planned a family dinner for the ninth which was Saturday since his birthday had fallen on a weekday and my brothers had to work. He loved ham so I made an Easter dinner. There's no sense in being ceremonial about holiday foods when a person is dying and can enjoy it without waiting for the actual holiday.

My aunt and cousin came by to see Dad for his birthday. Sophie came to take care of him as well and couldn't believe how good he looked. My Dad was impressed with her and they joked around and talked for a while. He forgot how hard it was for him to talk for a long time. My Aunt and Dad sang old Ukrainian songs. He remembered all the words. He even started to dance a little. He was so rejuvenated it was amazing to watch in awe this man who looked nearly dead just yesterday so full of life today. He told me that he breathes better when he sings.

On Friday, Pastor Tim came by to speak with my Dad. He brought him a bible and was speaking to him for a while. He asked my Dad, "Are you ready to go and stand before your Maker?" Dad answered, "Yes." They proceeded to talk a bit about God and then just general things. At this point I had left the room and didn't hear the rest of their conversation. That night, Guy and Dad read from the bible together before settling down for the night.

In the morning, I was preparing for the party. My Dad called us into the living room and said, "You know, I never knew God like this before. Sure I knew about Him and prayed but not in this way. God willing, if I'm still alive in the spring, I would like to go back to Europe and tell the people there because they don't know this either." A deep relief came over us. We knew that my Dad's eternity was now sealed. We knew that his faith was solid. We rejoice with him. I told the boys and DJ said, "only a year ago he was telling me not to talk too much about my faith so people wouldn't think I was a fanatic. I'm glad he now knows the truth".

My father asked me for a martini. He hadn't had a drink in a long time. He used to drink quite steadily. I asked his doctor and the doctor said give him whatever he wants if it makes him happy. I found out how to make a martini and gave it to him at his party. He raised his glass and gave a speech stating that he is so filled with happiness and warmth to have his family gathered around him like this. No matter what happens, he is ready and knows that for the end of his life his family had given him such great care, love, and happiness. He then drank his martini and complimented me on making such a fine drink! It was so clear that he was feeling happy that it just filled me to the core with joy.

My mom had gone for a lung scan two weeks ago. The doctor's office called her and said that the doctor would like to see her this week. We are squeezing you in for an appointment on November 13. My mother became anxious. Why would they be in such a rush to see her unless there was a problem. We also were going to a funeral home on Wednesday to pre-arrange for my father for when the time comes it would be less difficult if all the details are ironed out with a clear head.

Wednesday came and I told my father that I would be out with Mom for the afternoon. He said, "Oh, I'm going to miss you. When will you be home?"

"Around six."

"That late? Alright then. I love you."

"I love you too Daddy." and I left with my mom.

We first went to the funeral home. It was quite hard making arrangement for someone who was still living as if he were dead. It was dichotomous. I felt guilty. I literally felt like I was putting him in his grave. We filled out a pre-contract and said we would call them if we decide to have the funeral at their facilities. Our plan was to visit a few funeral homes since we still didn't know the area all that well and then make a decision on which one suited us best.

We headed over to my mother's doctor's office. We sat anxiously in the waiting room. When we were called in we both took a deep breath. The doctor came in quietly, shut the door, reviewed the chart, and then turned on the lights to read the x-rays. We waited. He turned to my mother and said, "Well,

it seems according to the x-rays that your lungs are clear."
We let out our breathes. Tears rolled down my cheeks. I was
relieved not to have my mother going through lung cancer too.
We grabbed a bite to eat on the way home and then I dropped
her off at her house.

When I got home, my Dad said, "I don't feel so well.
Maybe I should go to the hospital."

"What's wrong?"

"Just overall, I don't know."

Again I called the nurse and again she said to give him
anti-anxiety medicine. That evening it took a while before
it calmed him down and then he fell asleep. In the morning
he was again in that semi-conscious state although he could
speak but barely. He would ask to be pulled up so that I could
tap his back due to the feeling of phlegm in his lungs. He
didn't want to eat or drink. Mostly he slept. He would get up
to use the commode but needed assistance to walk. His legs
would collapse under him. I would try to form my questions
so that he could either nod yes or no.

The next day was the same. The home health aid started
coming daily. Our nurse said it would be any day now. I stood
in the kitchen and couldn't hold back the tears. They fell down
my cheeks like a storm. I was drowning in my own tears unable
to catch my breath. My father was dying right before my eyes
and there was nothing I could do. Nothing could help him. I
hadn't had a lot of time with him. It was only 5 weeks since he
had come to stay with us. I composed myself, prayed, and was
strengthened to do what I needed to do. I mentally prepared
myself as much as one can to endure and rise to the occasion.

The next morning he muttered that he wanted coffee. So I brought him a cup and he took only a few sips. He slept most of the time. He still would move his arms to gesture but his voice became weaker and it took too much effort for him to speak. Although he had a great command of the English language, he seemed to hear better if I spoke to him in Ukrainian. I called Ronnie and Tony and told them that he could go at any time and to come as soon as possible. Ronnie came and sat with him for most of Saturday.

Kathy from our church came by to take me out to lunch. I didn't want to leave. I was afraid to be away from him even for a minute. Instead she went and brought lunch home and we enjoyed while Ronnie sat with Dad. Kathy also had given me a baby monitor to place by his bed so that I could keep the receiver by my bed to be able to hear him through the night.

When Sophie came by, I was in the living room talking with Ronnie when I heard a blood curling yell coming from his room. "VICKY" my Dad had shouted. I ran into his room to see him sitting on the edge of the bed with Sophie holding him under one arm. He then whispered, "Help her". It was inaudible. Sophie said, "I think he wants you to help me bring him to the commode." A smile came over my face. This was just like Dad to use the little energy he had so that I could come and help Sophie. He wouldn't have yelled just for me to help him. I assisted her and left the room. Once he was back in bed, I came in. He lifted his arms up and I put my head on his chest. He wrapped his arms around me and kissed the top of my head several times as tears streamed from my eyes. It was such a small gesture that ended up being so special to me. Tony and his wife Martha came on Sunday. It was hard to see them torn up when they saw Dad in this condition.

DJ came in and Dad lifted up his arms and hugged him. He still wasn't speaking but was able to make slight gestures. We prayed with him. He folded his hands beneath his head and closed his eyes. We asked for forgiveness for any unrepented sin, for him to forgive anyone he still had anger toward, we asked for God to make his heart right with Him. We asked for a miracle and asked if a miracle wasn't in the plan that he wouldn't suffer.

The next day was Monday. Guy had taken the day off. Dad was in and out of consciousness. His arm movements were undistinguishable. He would lift his arms as if to gesture but they would be so heavy he would put them down. He no longer could nod but merely blink yes or no. He couldn't get out of bed although he would try when he needed the commode. I wasn't able to lift him at all. He was wearing diapers and we just had to deal with it. It seemed harder for him to deal with it. Pastor Joe came by to read Proverbs and to pray. He sat and talked with us for a while. I would continue talking to him assuming he could hear me. I reminisced about my precious childhood memories, I thanked him for always giving me positive reinforcement in everything I did, I told him how much the boys, Guy and I love him.

I had to drop water through a straw into his mouth which would then cause him to cough. He started to shakily grab at his sheets. I couldn't understand what he was trying to do. My thoughts raced. What if he thinks he is communicating fine and that I am just not helping him. What if he is screaming to me in his mind and thinks that he spoke. It would break my heart if his mind was working and his body wasn't and that he thought I was ignoring him. I would hold his hand and keep telling him I love him, I also told him it was okay to let go.

"I don't want to lose you Dad but I don't want you to suffer. Don't worry about us. We'll be okay. "

On Tuesday, Guy went to work for a little while but his boss sent him home and told him to stay with Dad for the time remaining. Dad just laid in bed motionless. He had bed sores that we would tend to, diapers to change, and I had moved over to using an oral sponge on a stick to dab water in his mouth. His eyes were open and lifeless. They didn't respond to light or movement. His hands were clasped over his stomach. The uvula at the back of his throat had shriveled down to a string from dehydration. His dentures no longer fit in his mouth for the same reason. I removed the dentures. It altered his appearance tremendously. Our visiting nurse and Sophie were coming every day now and couldn't believe that he was holding on for so long without food or water. On Wednesday, Sophie came by again.

She asked me, "Has everyone come to say goodbye?"

"Yes".

"What about your mother?"

"Oh no. She hasn't been by except once during the first week he was here. She wanted to give him his dignity. It also broke her heart to see him in this condition." "Besides, they have been divorced for a long time. I don't think he is waiting for her."

"Vicky, they were also married for a long time and share a rich history together. Maybe she needs to come."

"Well, I'll call her but you ask her."

No sooner did those words leave my mouth, than I heard my mother walk into my house.

"What's the matter?" my Mom asked.

I started crying. "We were just talking about you. Why are you here?"

"I felt I needed to be here for some reason. My Mom had not been here in weeks. Yet, today she felt an urging to come right at the moment that Sophie had suggested my Mom come to say goodbye.

I looked at Sophie and she asked my Mom. My Mom agreed. She walked in and sat down next to my father's bed as I looked on. She then grabbed his hand and caressed his face. The tears once again cascaded down my face. It's strange. At the age of 39 I was still touched to see my divorced parents together. I haven't seen them hold hands for over two decades. Yet, at the end of my Dad's life, I was given a gift. The gift was from my mother, my hero. She put aside any ills she may have carried and showed me her grace. I heard her call my father's name. She told him that he was a good man and there were no ill feelings anymore. She told him she was sorry that he had this horrible disease and that he was suffering. She told him that he was a good father. But that out of love for his children he has to let go. That the kids were all suffering watching him go through this. She spoke to him of the glory of heaven and the peace that he will have. She kissed his hand and stood up. She came out of the room and I ran to hug her. I needed my Mommy. I needed her strength. I needed her example! She held me while I cried. Sophie too was crying and hugged us. It was an undescribeable moment; too many emotions to even be able to try to convey. It was however, a moment that was perfect in action and timing.

We went into the living room. I said to my mother jokingly, 'Oh great, I bet Dad's thinking, I don't have to listen to you anymore, you are not my wife. I'll hang on as long as I want to hang on.' We laughed a much needed laugh. I could see that my mother was emotionally drained. So did Sophie. Sophie took my mother's shoes off and gave her a foot massage. Afterwards, my Mom said she was going to go home and lie down but would be here at any time if I needed her or if something happens. I thanked her and she left. Sophie gave me a hug and also left. I sat with Dad for most of the day. I had gospel music playing softly in the background for him. I and Guy would take turns reading the Psalms to him.

At around 10:00pm I knew I needed a distraction. I couldn't look at his lifeless body any longer. I came into the living room to sit and watch a comedy. Just as my body hit the sofa, my cat meowed relentlessly. "I must have locked her in my bedroom", I thought. I got up and went to my room. The door was wide open. I looked into my Dad's room which was caddy corner to mine and there was the cat. She was walking back and forth under my father's bed. I have this terrible habit of talking to my animals like June Lockhart on Lassie, so I said, "What are you telling me Ginger? Should I stay in here?" I sat down and she jumped in my lap as if to answer. I put my head down on my father's chest. About ten minutes later, his breathing stopped. I yelled, "Daddy, goodbye Daddy. Daddy, I love you", right into his ear at the top of my lungs. A feeling of helplessness had overcome me. He was leaving and I couldn't do anything. I so wanted to be with him at the time of his death and now that it was here, I was in a slight panic. I kept repeating "I love you, goodbye, goodbye Daddy." Guy and DJ ran into the room. They asked what's wrong and I told them he was gone. We just sat in silence for about 10 minutes, I was still laying on his chest crying when Guy said, "Vic, he's breathing again." I looked through my tears and could see the rise and fall of his chest. I said, "Thank you Daddy, thank you."

Guy and DJ stayed for a while and then went to bed. I went and told Tolyk about what happened and he said he wanted to stay with me in Dad's room until I was ready for bed. He brought his guitar in and played background music. Dad's breathing was strong. There was no Cheyne-Stokes breathing, no apnea, just a rhythmic breathing. At 1:00a.m. I told my Dad that I was going to bed but would be checking in on him periodically. Tolyk went to bed. I couldn't sleep. I thought I heard noises on the monitor and would jump up and run into his room every five minutes. By 1:45a.m. I said, "Dad, I'm going to bed. I won't check on you anymore. I'll see you in the morning. I love you." I kissed him and went to bed.

This time I did fall asleep. I jumped out of bed at 4:00a.m. for no reason at all and ran into his room. He was gone. There was a strange hue of blue around him. He's not here, I thought. I was calm. No tears. I gave him one last kiss and a last good-bye. I went and gently woke up Guy. He went into the room. I then woke DJ up and asked if he wanted to see him before I called the funeral home. He said no. Next, I went to Tolyk and asked him. He got out of bed and came in the room and quickly walked out. I called Samaritan. Within an hour, the on-call nurse came out and checked his vitals. She then instructed me to flush all his medications. I then called the funeral home. I called and told my brothers that Dad had passed away. After an hour, the people from the funeral home arrived. I gave them all the information and then excused myself. I didn't want to watch them carry him out in a bag. After they left I called my brothers. I told them I would update them with the funeral arrangements later in the afternoon. I then called my mother and told her. She cried. I called my aunt and she cried. After I finished all my calls, I sat down in the rocking chair. I felt a warmth suddenly envelope my body. I was filled once again with a peace that surpasses all understanding, His peace. This time however, I could feel it physically. I was overcome with joy. I pictured my father gazing at the face of Jesus. He had his new body. He knew who shot JFK. All thoughts of warmth and comfort overcame me. It was inexplicable.

After a couple of hours, we went over to the funeral home and made all the arrangements. I was calm. I was almost professional about it. I tear escaped my eye when I picked out prayer cards but that was all. My father requested to be cremated and then his remains were up to us. There would be no funeral. I had thought to perhaps sprinkle them over the mountains of his hometown in Ukraine to honor him but I would need to discuss it with my brothers.

When we came home, Guy called our church. Our pastor told us that the church would take care of the reception and that we need not worry. Kathy and Donna from church would do all the shopping, cooking, and preparing so that after the services we could come home and not have to lift a finger. I was so touched. That was love. Guy went to go get the mail. He came back in with a brown package.

As he opened it he said, "Vic, we got a package from WAWZ, the radio station that I had volunteered for a few weeks ago."

"What is it?" I asked.

"It's a gift for volunteering. A cd of the Book of John."

"That's nice."

"Don't you get it?"

Stunned, I said, "Yeah, they sent you a cd of the book of John for volunteering your time. Why are you so excited?"

"Vic, I volunteered a month ago. Don't you find it interesting that on the day that Dad died they sent us the book of John which is what I was reading to him?"

I gasped. "God sent us a receipt. He has Dad!" Out of all the things the radio station could have sent us; t-shirts, bumper stickers, music cd's, it seemed to be no coincidence that He sent us the book of John on the day of my father's arrival in heaven.

On Friday, I prepared the collages with pictures of my Dad from early childhood to more recent pictures. I cleaned the house. I was exhausted. I shed no more tears. My grieving had happened well before he died. It started the day we learned he had cancer.

There were more phone calls to make and as I was on the phone I looked out into the pasture and saw smack in the middle of the field, one of our goats nursing two brand new baby goats! A sign of rebirth came to mind, life more abundantly. Life is important to God.

Saturday was the viewing. The collages turned out to be a nice memorial to my father. Flowers filled the room. I placed a rose in my father's hands. I should have placed it in his teeth since he and my Mom used to love to tango but thought that would be in bad taste. My brother gave a beautiful eulogy emphasizing the need to honor our loved ones while they are still with us. Pastor Tim gave a sermon underlining the need to know God because life is unpredictable. Many people came to support us that didn't even know my father.

My brother Ronnie was having a difficult time seeing my father in the casket. I stood between my two brothers in the first row. I took turns hugging them making sure I gave equal time to each. As the youngest and only girl of the family I had taken on a new role of care giver since my mother's open heart surgery and now with having taken on caring for my father. The strength was not of my own. I know it came from faith. Each time I needed more faith I prayed for it–and received it!

As we left the funeral home, Guy and I were the last to leave. I stopped at the door, glanced at my father lying in the casket, I touched my fingers to my lips, blew him a kiss and whispered, "Goodbye Daddy, goodbye."

Once at the house, there was more food than I could imagine. Kathy and Donna worked tirelessly with huge smiles on their faces. They were truly humble servants to my family and guests. Many of our guests wanted to see the room that my father had died in. I found this curious. Tony was amazed by the generosity of the church and the fact that Kathy and Donna were so willing to prepare all the food and serve it to our guests. He said, "this shows me the heart of Christianity more than any sermon ever could." He was right. This was Kathy and Donna walking the walk. It was a visual not an audio. Many have the gift of speech but their lifestyles contradict the words. This was a great witness to my brother. Again, I was seeing God working in our lives.

On Sunday evening we took the boys to the movies. On the way home we heard one of my favorites Christian songs on the radio. We turned it up and started singing. Then it hit me. The words suddenly were more than just a song. It was "I Can Only Imagine" by MercyMe. I cried. They were tears of joy because I could only imagine my Dad walking on the streets of gold. I really tried to picture heaven for the first time since I was a child. Having my father in heaven somehow made it even more real to me. It seemed to make it more attainable. Not that I ever doubted it, it's just that now it was no longer in black and white but in color for me.

About a week later I was stricken with a severe migraine/sinus headache. My bottom teeth hurt. First I went to my dentist. The x-rays didn't reveal any problems so I went to my regular doctor, I was given strong narcotics for the pain. This caused me to vomit violently and restricted me to the couch. I was typically healthy and yet felt so miserable. Again, thoughts went to my father. I started to have a better understanding of the effects his medication must have had on him and he was in such a weakened state. Yet, he proved to be such a trooper. No complaining, still concerned for everyone else. Not me. All I could think of was how horrible I felt. Christmas was just around the corner and I couldn't start decorating or baking because I was so miserable.

A week and a half went by and I still couldn't get off the couch. I went back to the doctor. By this time the right side of my face had swollen so much that it was hard to diagnose. He said first I'll send you to an ear, nose, and throat specialist, if that doesn't resolve this, go to the dentist. So I went to the specialist. He must have been a sadist. He took the back of a metal instrument and stretched out my already swollen cheek another few inches. Then he tapped hard on my teeth. I thought I saw my Dad calling me toward the light. He then said he thought it was a dental issue. He recommended a local dentist so after my head stopped swimming from the pain of his smack, I went. The dentist again took an x-ray. Still nothing showed up. But due to the swelling she was able to trace it back to two teeth. She said she would try to guess which one needed root canal. I said, "fine" do as many root canals you want until you fix this. I can't take it anymore. Once she started drilling, it was clear that she had the right tooth. I immediately felt relieve until she handed me the bill for which I had no money. It also turned out that our health insurance had again been cancelled due to Guy's company not paying the premium. We now had another $900.00 worth of debt that we didn't know how to pay. Not to mention, no money for Christmas.

I was doing much better. A friend came by for bible study and gave us an early Christmas gift. Money to buy the boys presents. Just when I thought we had run out of our quota of blessings, God poured them out on us again. Kathy from church had also been busy. She had sent out a letter to people she knew explaining our plight and asking for any help that they were willing to donate. One woman donated hand blown glass ornaments for me to be able to give out as gifts. Others sent small checks which quickly added up. Our Christmas gift problem was solved. Even some of our smaller bills could be paid.

We were looking forward to the New Year. We wanted to put this year behind us, far behind us. We had great hopes for the New Year. On New Year's Eve, Guy took me to select a new puppy for my 40th birthday which was the next day. We brought her home and I went to Wall-Mart to get supplies. In the parking lot, my cell phone rang. It was Guy calling from home probably with a request for a few more things. "Vic, where are you?"

"At wall-mart what do you need?"

"Come home."

"What's the matter?"

"DJ was in a car accident on the New Jersey Parkway."

"I'm on my way." DJ and his friends had car pooled up to North Jersey to do some rock climbing near our old hometown. His friend Jenn drove his car with three other girls, and DJ was in Dan's car with Dan's brother Matt. I didn't know the severity of the accident, just that it would take us over an hour to get to him. On my way home, I called my mom and told her. A few minutes later, Tony called and said he and his wife would drive out to the accident since he was only about 20 minutes away from there.

I got home and Guy and I drove up. He told me that no one was hurt but Jenn was very shaken up. Apparently DJ's car was most likely totaled.. I called DJ on his cellphone. He said Jenn didn't have her license. Jenn was from Canada. She also didn't have her passport with her. This was going to be complicated, I thought. He explained that a car had cut Jenn off causing her to slam on her brakes and rear end the car. Dan also rear ended Jenn who was driving DJ's car. The first car fled the scene. Once we arrived, they were just about to tow away DJ's car. We wouldn't be able to get it until Jan. 2 due to the holiday. Jenn was hysterically crying and apologizing. We told her it was an accident and only metal. We were grateful everyone was alright. I then went to DJ and just held him. Tony and Martha were trying to comfort Jenn and the other girls. They had to leave because they had dinner reservations and just wanted to make sure that someone was with the kids until we arrived.

The state police issued a ticket to both Jenn and Dan and left. Dan's car was driveable so DJ and the girls all jumped into our van and we headed home. We sang songs the whole way just to calm everyone down but only after we gave our thanks to the Lord for His hand of protection on our children. It could have been so much worse, that was clear based on the damage of DJ's car.

Our neighbors were having a New Year's Eve party for the youth group. At midnight they would administer communion and sing praise songs. We headed over there and enjoyed the rest of the night.

Chapter Nine
Waiting on the Lord

January was peaceful. Guy received a paycheck on January 15th and on the 30th, just like in the old days. I also received a small check from my father's life insurance.

My mother had been diagnosed with gallstones a few weeks ago but the pain was getting progressively worse. We spoke to a surgeon and he scheduled her for surgery on January 28th. We went to the cardiologist to receive clearance for surgery. He said she was a high risk patient for a low risk surgery. We debated whether or not the surgery was safe. Yet, her pains increased and there were no other options. Her gallstones were too large. The surgery would be laproscopic which would be only about one hour long. If they came across a problem then it would require a more invasive surgery resulting in a four hour procedure putting her at a much higher risk. We decided on having the surgery and a lot of prayer.

The day of her surgery arrived. Guy, Tony, and I waited with trepidation. An hour later the surgeon came out and said she was doing fine. Relief filled the air. Pastor Joe came by in the evening to pray with her. She was released the next morning and needed to take it easy for one week. For now all was well.

During that week, I received a phone call from the mall ministry. Elsie, the director, had asked me if I would be interested in teaching their Evangelism Class. My first inclination was to say no, then the prompting came. 'This isn't about you Vicky. This is about the gifts I gave you.' I thought about it. Why am I hesitant? I currently teach a bible study and computer class. I understand evangelism. What was holding me back? Self-doubt. I felt I needed to be obedient since I believed I was called to do this and finally agreed. I was being taken out of my comfort zone but not unprepared. All the components were there. I wasn't going into this alone.

We applied for FEMA because all of our funds have run out. The college education accounts for DJ and Tolyk had been depleted. It was now a year and a half after 9/11. Most people had moved on. We were asked frequently, "Why doesn't Guy just find another job?" There were several answers to that question. First, the job market was not so conducive due to the economy. Secondly, we had a year and a half of back pay invested in his company. If he walked away now there was a chance that either he wouldn't receive the back pay or it would be low on the priority list. Thirdly, there was a determination by the employees and employer to not be defeated by terrorists. It was a camaraderie that has developed through this crisis. They were all determined to make this work. James the owner of the company had been advised to file chapter 11. This would give him a fresh start and not need to payback the employees. He refused. He had more loyalty to his employees than that.

February brought another paycheck. We were able to catch up on December's and January's bills. March was uneventful.

On April 9th I went out to give the animals their evening feeding and noticed two of the goats were lying down and moaning. They did not respond to the food. I ran into the house to get Guy and by the time we came back, one had died. Guy jumped on the internet to look up any remedies and found baking soda to be a solution. He went out and administered this to the other goat who was near death at this point. Within thirty minutes she was back on her feet and eating.

The next morning, our horse was lying down and having trouble getting up. We finally were able to get him up and into his stall. He then fell down to the ground and was struggling to get up to no avail. I called the vet and they suggested he might be colic. However, he was not showing the typical symptoms of colic. When the vet arrived, he listened to his heart and said that his heart was in fibrillation. I waited for the recommended treatment. He just stood there. "Doc, what do we do now?"

"If we could get him to a hospital, get him on some machines and give him treatment, there still is no guarantee that he might not go back into fibrillation. This would also run you a couple of thousand dollars."

"What other options are there?"

He just stared.

"Euthanasia?"

"I'm afraid so."

"Oh no. Okay doc just give me a minute with him." It was hard to do. When the animals die for whatever reasons, it's somehow easier to accept than when you have to make the decision. Although I knew there were no other options, it's painful when you have to decide to end a life. I went into the stall and crouched down next to him. I petted him and tried to soothe him. I felt horrible. As I soothed him I realized I was comforting him only to have to put him down. I started to cry. I walked out. The doctor walked in. After a few minutes, the doctor came out and said, "he's gone." Another chapter closed in our lives. Another loss . Each event felt like an arrow piercing us, yet not fatally. Our next step was to call a company to come and remove him. By the end of the day, he was gone. Our other horse, Silver, (we are not very original) searched the property line for him and then just quietly settled into his stall for the night.

The next day, DJ was going to the cell phone store to replace the phone he lost two months ago. He took Tolyk with him. Being a bit nervous whenever he was on the road, I asked him to call me and let me know when he gets to the store.

When the phone rang, DJ wanted to know which phone he should select. Ten minutes later he called to ask what plan would be best to purchase. Fifteen minutes later, the phone rang again.

"Mom, I just wanted to let you know we couldn't buy the phone without you to sign for it. We're leaving now."

"Ok sweetheart. Be careful."

"I will."

As usual, I said a quick prayer of protection. Five minutes later the phone rang again. This time it was Tolyk.

"Mom. Get down to the Honda dealer fast."

"Why?"

"We were just in a wreck." He said breathlessly.

"Okay." My heart was in my throat. Guy was standing next to me.

"The boys were just in a car accident." I grabbed my keys and we ran out the door. I wasn't even thinking clearly. I didn't even ask if they were okay. I just knew I had to get there and was starting to shake. We drove in silence. We pulled up into the parking lot and there was DJ's car. The whole front of his car looked like a crushed soda can. I scanned the parking lot for the boys. Finally my eyes rested on them near the police car. They were both standing. Thank you Lord. I ran to Tolyk who was closer and hugged him. He said, "Go to DJ, he's really shaken up." I ran over to DJ and just grabbed him and held him. He was shaking. I held him tightly and whispered, "Are you alright?"

"I guess so. My chest hurts. I'm sorry Mom, I'm so sorry."

"It's okay honey. What happened?" I asked.

"We were driving down the highway at about 55mph. I looked at Tolyk for only a second and when I looked back the car in front of me had switched lanes and the next thing I saw was a pickup truck stopped still. There wasn't enough time to come to complete stop but I tried. We slammed into the back of the truck as he was waiting to make a turn into the dealership. The airbags had deployed from the impact."

I gasped. He hit a truck that wasn't moving at 55 miles per hour! Why Lord? I had prayed for his protection! Yet he was involved in an accident. The answer then came to me. It seemed that the Lord said, "And I protected him!" I cried. He did. He really did. They were so blessed to even be alive. This was later confirmed by the insurance adjuster. I went over to the other driver, who was kind of rough looking and said I was sorry. He then told me that he had had no idea that he was struck. He thought that he had dropped his transmission. The boys told me he was really nice to them and kept asking if they were alright. The policeman was kind also. He didn't issue DJ a ticket. He also suggested we go to the hospital. DJ was having chest pains and Tolyk's knee had slammed into the dashboard.

As we left for the hospital the other driver said, "Just take care of your car. I'll fix my truck myself. Don't worry about it." They couldn't have run into a nicer person.

"Thank you. God bless you." They were discharged from the hospital the same night. There were no punctures on DJ's x-ray. It was most likely bruising from the seatbelt and some of the pain from anxiety. Tolyk had a minor injury. His knee was inflamed. He needed an immobilizer and to keep it iced.

Once Tolyk was able to go back to school, I stopped at the Taco Bell after dropping him off. I was lost in thought. It had been a difficult month. I was weighted down by all the events. My thoughts were interrupted by the screech of the drive-thru speaker. "Your order comes to $2.37. Please pull up to the first window." As I drove around to the window, I realized I didn't have any money with me. It was at home. I told the server what had happened with embarrassment and asked him to cancel my order.

"How much do you have with you?"

"About fifty-three cents."

"Don't worry about it."

"No. It's okay. I can't let you do that."

"One day when I tell you I'm thirsty, you'll give me something to drink"

I gasped. Did I hear him right? Was he quoting scripture to me?

"Excuse me?." I said, thinking I must not have heard him correctly."

"One day when I tell you I'm thirsty, you'll give me something to drink."

I was stunned. "Thank you so much. God bless you."

"You too." he said smiling as I drove away in bewilderment. I've imprinted that on my heart and know that "one of the least of these" can come in many forms. I owe this to God. I need to be alert lest I miss the opportunity to give a drink to the thirsty.

The new school was working hard to raise funds. For many nights after work, Guy went over to the building to help fix it up and set up a computer lab. We handed out information on the school hoping to increase enrollment. We also ran a garage sale with the proceeds going to the building fund. When the Farm Fair rolled around we had a booth for a few days advertising the school and answering any questions. Guy started a letter writing campaign to local Christians and organizations as well as friends and family who might want to donate. His office donated a very expensive and sophisticated phone system to the school. He worked night after night to help insure that the school would open as scheduled in September. I was approached for a teaching job. They still needed an English teacher. I was excited at the prospect but was hesitant because Principal Y was already micro managing even the simplest things.

We had a small barbeque over the weekend. Our former Pastor, Joe and family attended. His wife and I talked for some time. She explained that her good friend and colleague had just lost her teaching job. She went on to explain the situation and before she could finish I explained to her that God was in this conversation. I said, "What are the chances that we could come together today for an impromptu barbeque and that you would bring with you this burden about your friend?" I continued to tell her that I had an exciting opportunity for her friend at a groundbreaking new Christian High School. We exchanged contact information. It was amazing to see God solve two problems with one conversation. It was also exciting to be an instrument for Him. Before long, her friend went to the interview and was accepted as the new English teacher.

Tolyk's knee was still giving him problems. We went to the orthopedic surgeon again. This time he said Tolyk would need surgery. His knee was too unstable and would be susceptible to reinjuries and dislocations. The surgery was scheduled for June 20th . This way it would be after school was out. Four days before surgery, he was afflicted with poison ivy all over his legs. By the time of the surgery, the poison ivy had dried up although it was quite visible. We mentioned it to the surgeon who said we couldn't do the surgery. He left the room. He returned and stated, "Rub your legs with alcohol to dry it out and we'll do the surgery." Tolyk remained awake during the procedure and was allowed to watch it. He was fascinated by the technology. After 45 minutes, the surgery is over. He was setup with crutches, prescriptions, instructions bandages, and then sent home. He wanted to go out for lunch and bore the pain very well without any medications. After several weeks, he was scheduled for physical therapy three times a week for eight weeks. Halfway through the therapy, he had a follow up visit with the surgeon. The doctor said his knee is completely healed and that he could stop physical therapy. Amazing! Gratitude filled my heart that he was healed so quickly.

When July rolled around we knew we needed a vacation. Although, money was tight, it was a matter of shall we go on a trip or pay for some intensive therapy. We decided that a vacation would be cheaper and probably more effective for us. We went to a ranch in North Carolina that my parents had discovered before I was born. I had gone there many times as a child and the beauty of it has always had me longing to go back from time to time. I was glad to be able to share it with the boys and Guy since this was a treasured childhood place for me.

The ranch sits in a sloping valley of the Blue Ridge Parkway and not far from the Smoky Mountains. The aroma of Mountain Laurel fills the air as you drive up the winding road.

There is a panoramic view of the mountains in the backdrop that stand majestically enveloping the ranch. The ranch itself seems untouched by time. The rooms are in small houses spread out over the property. Although the rooms do furnish a television and an air conditioner, most modern amenities are absent. Since there are only three channels that come in slightly snowy, it pushes you out to enjoy God's creation. There are no phones in the room (what a blessing) and a bell is rung to alert you to three scrumptious home-cooked, southern style meals a day. People pass you and say "Hey" not antagonistically but rather as a greeting. A lake adorns the premises as does a built-in, spring fed pool.

Babbling brooks are heard all around as you walk down to the dining hall. Trails for hiking abound or if you are so inclined, you can saddle up on a horse for these trails at a nominal fee. I took many hikes up to the mountain time during our stay there. Yes, you really can commune best with God from a mountain top. Not because somehow you're a few miles closer to Him, but because you have left everything manmade and are completely surrounded by His creation. The mountains, the forest animals, the sky, and the crisp mountain air. There are no distractions. On the mountain everything is in sync. There doesn't seem to be any chaos. That peacefulness washes over you.

There is much to do in the area or nothing to do. It's a personal choice. Compared to some of the Orlando trips we have taken, this was the most peaceful and relaxing vacation we have had in a long time. We met some interesting people from all over the country who also know the secret location of this beautiful ranch. We enjoyed everything from the ambience to the food and even ourselves. But it was time to return to the

21st century and our lives. We drove the 11 hours back home refreshed from our trip and ready for the next chapter of our lives.

Shopping for dormitory supplies consumed us for the next couple of weeks. It was necessary to buy a little at a time as our funds would allow. Fortunately DJ's roommate was bringing a refrigerator and my father had left me his microwave so that took all the big ticket items off our shoulders. Yet, it seemed amazing to me how expensive everything was. Maybe it was just because I had a budget and couldn't buy at will. I was very conscience of the prices and how to stick to only the necessities for now. A gloominess started to set in as I realized that my first born baby was now leaving home to begin the rest of his life. Excitement filled me at the opportunities ahead of him and the wonderful environment he would experience at Liberty University. Yet, I wasn't ready to let go (not emotionally anyway). He was making his way to adulthood and his need for me was being diminished. I was losing my identity. For the last 18 years I was a mother which includes the gamut of care giver, teacher, tutor, typist, role model, advisor, chef, baker, banker, nurse, launderer, maid, taxi driver, class mother, cub scout leader, cheerleader, counselor, comforter, etc. I was losing my job!

There would be cutbacks. I would still be banker, and maybe work in shipping and handling college care packages, but not much more. Others would be taking over my roles. My mind went back to his childhood. Remembering the many hugs and kisses, questions he asked because he thought I knew everything, the boo-boos that I could heal with a mere kiss caused my eyes to leak. What if he doesn't come back home after college? A plethora of fearful questions once again invaded my thinking. I shook my head and continued to pack up his things. Instead, I forced myself to focus on the positives; the friends he would make, the Christian fellowship that would enfold him. A smile crept onto my face. This was better. Focus on the positive I told myself.

As we loaded up the car and jumped in on our way to the university, a song came on the radio. It was a country song about how when our children are little we can't wait until they grow older, we pray for their dreams to come true...and they do. Well that did it. I sobbed with my whole being down the highway. Guy said, "Honey just change the station," and through my tears I said, "It's okay. I love this song." He just shook his head. It was just one of those times he couldn't understand why I didn't take his solution. For me it was one of those times when I didn't want a solution. As we drove for the next six hours, we had mostly country stations on the radio since we were heading south. It just so happened that that song was on the top 40 and was playing on all the stations at varying times. Ugh. All this crying is going to give me a headache, I thought.

Guy had taken an alternate route to cut down our travel time. So instead of our trip being 6 hours it ended up being 8 hours. Tired of crying and just plain tired, we pulled up by the dorms and unloaded. I took all the necessary pictures of the dorm hall, the dorm room door with his name on it, his roommate, and his room. We left him to go and settle into our hotel room. The weekend went well and DJ had all the provisions he needed. We sat in on the family orientation program at the college. They assured us that they know that we are entrusting our children to them to be well cared for both physically and spiritually. I felt comforted. They seemed to understand a mother's heart. They discussed the concerns that most parents have letting their children go away from home and I finally started to have peace. This was going to be alright. He was in good hands. They went further to say that many of their students have found their future spouses from all across the country while in college. I'm taking him home I thought. He can't marry somebody from the other side of the country. Besides, next year when Tolyk comes here, there's the off chance that he might meet someone from yet another state. My quandary would then be 'where do I live?' I can't pick between my children. No. This was not acceptable. I whispered my concerns to Guy. He basically humored me and said, "if the girls they chose are truly good Christians they will be subservient wives and will go where the boys go, which naturally would be close to you." I still wasn't confident. I decided to table it for now although the concept of pre-arranged marriage was somehow appealing.

The trip home went well except that we were short one family member. It would now only be the three of us for a while, a difficult concept. I felt incomplete but knew that I would have to adapt.

Chapter Ten
Put Not Your Trust in Men

During the summer, the school was taking applications for spiritual leadership officer positions. Principal X strongly encouraged Tolyk to submit an application because she felt that he had great leadership qualities. It had taken time but Tolyk overcame the disappointment of the other school closing and had now renewed his mind. He was to be a pioneer. He would rise to leadership. This would be his year. He submitted his application. He was also informed that Principal X and Principal Y are the ones who determine the officer positions. He was excited.

The school year started. He signed up for soccer. There was hope that he would receive a scholarship for soccer. He was made captain. He also was on the yearbook committee, and was leading worship. After many practices and a few games, the team decided to cancel the season since attendance for practice was sparse.

The results of the elections were in. As a senior in a class of five, we assumed he would make president. As I picked him up from school, I enthusiastically asked, "So, what position did you get?"

"None."

"What do you mean?"

"I didn't receive any of the officer positions."

"Why would they do that to you?"

"That's what I would like to know."

We drove home in silence. He was so crestfallen. He had such high hopes and such a positive attitude about this year and what he would do and now his dreams lay shattered at his feet.

Two days later, I received a call from the school. I was required to come in for a meeting. The nature of the meeting was a result of a homework policy they had implemented in the beginning of September. I appreciated the policy. If a student missed one homework assignment, the teacher called the parents. If he missed two assignments, the parent gets punished. I mean, the parent comes in for a meeting. But I viewed this meeting in a positive light. This would be my opportunity to discuss the elections.

Once at the school, we discussed Tolyk's homework habits. Once we finished I broached the spiritual leadership topic.

"Principal X, I have a concern to discuss with you. Tolyk told me how you had encouraged him to submit an application for spiritual leadership and how you continued to encourage him and sharing your vision of his leadership qualities."

"Yes, I felt he would be a great leader."

"Why then would you set him up for failure?"

"I didn't set him up for failure. We decided he wasn't ready for a leadership role."

How can you change your mind after you pretty much guaranteed him that he would have the position? Besides, he's a senior, this was his last opportunity to be involved. He had been through so much these last couple of years. He was deathly ill from Lymes Disease, 9/11 and the repercussions of that, getting jumped at his other school, then the Christian school closing, losing his grandfather, and now this. Don't you understand that he is at the end of his hope. To a teenager, this is tramatic.

"We just felt that his skills could be used elsewhere."

"Like?"

"Like as a music ministry leader. He would be solely responsible for selecting worship music and leading the group in worship with his guitar"

"Well I think that's great but you already told him he had that role."

"That's the best we could do."

"Thank you for your time."

Okay, there was nothing else that could really be said. After all, they couldn't just manifest a pseudo position for him nor would he want that. The positions were already filled. Lord help me to help my child. I felt like I failed him in this meeting. I was starting to think that as much as we had pumped up this school for him that we had overestimated the joy. By the time I reached home Tolyk was just hanging up the phone. It was a friend of his from school who also didn't get a spiritual leadership position. Evidently they created a pseudo position for him because his parents hemmed and hawed enough.

"So what position did I get?" he asked.

"None. Sorry son. I couldn't reach them."

"No problem. I'm not surprised. I don't think that Principal Y likes me anyway."

Soon basketball season was starting up. They still didn't have a coach. Tolyk naturally approached Guy and he agreed. They started practice. It was a nice diversion for Guy since it had been two months without a paycheck again and Christmas was approaching. Christmas was modest once again. The first day back at school after Christmas break, we received a letter in the mail. It was from the school. Our December payment was late. It was the first time since school started. The letter basically stated that payment had to be made before returning to school in January. If payment was not received by then, Tolyk could not attend school and that this point was not negotiable.

They would not work with us. To throw away six remaining months of tuition which is $2400 merely because this one payment was late by three weeks was inconceivable to me. Secular companies give you a grace period. Credit card companies work with you, but not the school that we helped start. We were all mortified. We couldn't help but surmise that they didn't want Tolyk there. Why? Why mask it as a financial issue. We spoke with another student who told us that they offered her a scholarship due to her inability to afford the school. Yet for us we are told that he can't attend due to non-payment! We started to become outraged. They were well aware of our extenuating circumstances but wouldn't work with us. We were at our breaking point. This is his senior year. He can't be uprooted again. I racked my brain trying to figure out what to do. We didn't want him to go back to the public high school and there weren't any affordable Christian high schools in the area. Stress doesn't describe how we felt. It appeared our proverbial house of cards was tenaciously close to tumbling.

We had until January 12th to pay for December and now January's payment or else he would not be welcomed back. At this point Tolyk didn't want to go back. He felt that Principal Y didn't like him and was trying to find a way to get him out of the school.

I looked into home school options. It was important to me to find an accredited homeschool academy. I wasn't sure how he would handle homeschooling. It would require a lot of discipline on his part. This was all new to me and I wasn't quite sure how to implement a homeschool program. After many phone calls, hours on the net, and help from some homeschool moms, we found an academy. There were only two problems. One was that since we had never homeschooled through their academy before, we would have to pay for the whole year and that he would have to do the work in the program from September through June. The second problem was that it would cost us $1200 dollars. Once again, I approached my mom for assistance. As a retired senior citizen on a limited income, she is extremely giving which has always been her way. Years of sacrificing for me I thought had come to an end.

Yet here I am again turning to her for help. We had a season where I was able to do for her for a while but that season ended on 9/11/01.

The school notified us that someone, anonymously, was willing to pay the remainder of his tuition. We discussed it with Tolyk, but he had resigned himself to homeschooling and believed that if he were to return it would just be a matter of time before they found another reason to oust him but now at someone else's expense.

In two weeks we were up and running. We had a program for the computer and that seemed to be the appropriate media for a teenager. Without much cajoling, Tolyk was up at 8:30 and diligently working through the day until 2:30 with an hour for lunch. He was motivated, he was learning, he was in control of his education, and was doing great.

Because Tolyk had attended the first four days of January, the former school wanted a partial payment. We didn't have to pay for December because each month was prepaid which started in August. However, the first four days was basically turning in his books, cleaning out his locker and saying goodbye. They released unofficial transcripts without grades and without recognition for soccer, yearbook, worship, and basketball. It didn't matter since we were starting the year over with the homeschool academy but it would have been nice to have the added accolades.

Adding insult to injury, the school decided to obliterate any trace of my son from the yearbook. All group pictures were photoshopped to remove him. Although he was the soccer captain and the season was now over, he was erased and another person was placed in the role of captain under false pretenses. The extent to which they had gone to erase him from being affiliated with the school was beyond comprehension. What crime did he commit that he deserved this? Clearly this went beyond being late on tuition.

Our hearts were wounded, our minds were full of resentment, our spirits were weary, and yet we needed to go on. Our prayer was that our faith would supercede the pain and create pleasing meditations unto the Lord. We needed to release the offense. A struggle in the flesh that was so fresh and hard to let go of. We needed our Christian brothers and sisters to stand alongside us. This felt like being sideswiped in a car because we never expected this. Another difficulty was explaining to our unsaved friends and family how a Christian school, knowing our situation, was not willing to work with us. Regardless, he was tenacious and was able to do an entire school year through this online academy in five months. His grades were very high and he had finished school. Unfortunately, he had no alma mater as a result of three schools letting him down. The homeschool association allowed him to graduate with them and he did so reluctantly. He was becoming soured towards Christians and I suspect he just wanted to be done with this chapter of his life and move on to college life. In the fall, he too would be attending Liberty University.

Summer of 2004 was eventful as if we needed more of that in our lives. DJ came home from college with a friend to work at the Christian Camp nearby. One day, the phone rang and it was news of my cousin who lived in Ukraine. He recently had moved to Russia with the hopes of finding work there. After the fall of the U.S.S.R., the economy was suffering and jobs were very scarce. However, he was unaware of the red tape involved in moving his pension over from one country to another. So his wife travelled back to Ukraine to straighten out the paperwork. Upon her return, she found a letter that he left for her. (Very few people had telephones.) He told her that he had made two trips to the hospital while she was away because of some stomach problems. They could not do anything for him so they sent him home. This time it was so severe that he was going back to the hospital anyway. She returned on a Friday and went immediately to the hospital to see him. When she arrived, she spoke with him and he assured her that he would be fine. He was more worried about her having travelled so far and needing to get some rest. He told her to come back the next morning. She did as he asked. After a good night's rest, she returned to the hospital but her husband was not in his room. She kept asking for him but the nurses ignored her. Finally a man walking down the hallway, maybe a doctor, he heard my cousin's name, and, over his shoulder informed her nonchalantly that he had passed away. The man never looked back at her nor did he stop walking. She broke down and cried.

It turned out that my cousin had peritonitis and needed a strong antibiotic. Additionally, he needed to have his abdomen drained of this infection. Unfortunately, there were no doctors on duty at the time because it was the weekend and evening time. So he died, an avoidable death because no one would tend to him. Only a short time earlier, my other cousin, his brother, died from a brain tumor. All of my mother's blood relatives, were gone now. The only remaining cousin was a woman whom my aunt had adopted. She too, has a tragic story to tell.

A few weeks later, I was gardening outside and it was a very humid day. I came into the house at around 6:00p.m. for a glass of water when the phone rang. Not meaning any disrespect to my mother, I was debating whether or not to answer it because it could involve a long political discussion. After all, I had only come in to get a drink, I could have been outside and then not heard the phone ring. Well, my conscience got the best of me and I answered the phone. On the other end, my mother spoke in a weak, but panicked voice, "Vicky come quick, I've had an accident". My mind was trying to process the information. "What kind of accident, where are you?" My mother replied, "I fell, on the cement in front of my house". "I'm on my way". Once again, I believe that God prompted me to respond to the call since I am her only contact. Guy and I jumped in the car, Tolyk wanted to come too but we told him to stay because it would be too much confusion for my mother. On the way, we called 911. When we got there, she was laying on the cement walk in front of her door. By the way she was laying, Guy and I having both been first responders in the past, assessed that she may have a broken hip. When the ambulance arrived, they tried to figure out a way to lift her up. She was writhing in pain with each attempt. We tried to tell them that she may have a broken hip. They were going to scoop her up quickly but we insisted that they stop. Then they wanted to try and straighten out her leg and Guy stopped them telling them that it may be broken and they would do more damage. Finally, we convinced them to use an instrument called a scoop minimizing the movement involved.

Once at the hospital, she was in extreme pain and we begged a nurse to give her medicine while she waits for the doctor. It was a busy evening in the emergency room and she could be suffering a long time. The medicine did not abate the pain completely but seemed to just bring it down a notch. The E.R. had her get x-rays which is always a problem when you have a broken bone and need to lie down in unnatural positions. She was in tears from the manipulations as they wheeled her out of the x-ray room. It was determined that she had broken her hip and part of her femur as well as her shoulder in the fall. Since she is a cardiac and pulmonary patient, it was a huge risk factor for her to have surgery. Conversely, since it was both her hip and shoulder on the same side, she would lose functionality of those limbs, drastically changing her life. She first needed cardiac clearance so they put her on strong medications, and the next day would have the cardiologist come in for a consult at the hospital.

The next day, the cardiologist came in and determined that the risks did not outweigh the benefits. She would be treated as a high risk patient but would receive clearance for surgery. I called the surgeon several times trying to gather as much information as possible to help me finalize my decision and hers. Finally, we decided to proceed with surgery.

God was merciful and spared my Mom. She stayed a few days at the hospital and then was transferred to a rehabilitation center for the next ten weeks. The medications were not so merciful. She became not only loopy but had hallucinations from the medicines. Yet, I watched as she asked the nurse what each of the pills were and then would arbitrarily select one that she has decided she would not take. It was interesting that the mind was still telling her to be vigilant and careful in her medical care but she did not have the wherewithal to really process the names and purposes of the medications.

She was lucid a lot of the times but when the pain increased and the stronger pain killers were administered, she became a different person.

I received a call one night at around 1:00a.m. to come to the hospital. She was pulling out all of her I.V.'s and was having paranoid delusions. She thought that the staff was trying to hurt her and she wanted me to take her away. She recognized me, which was good, but she also thought she could still walk. In her memory, she remembered that she had had hip and shoulder surgery at some point, but that it was in the past and this was a completely different scenario. She kept trying to get out of bed and tell me she'll walk me to the door (she thought she was in her old house where I was born). Finally, she became tired from the medications and fell asleep.

One elderly man comes to the rehabilitation center when they opened the doors at 7:30a.m. He stays all day by his wife's side until 8:30p.m. I asked him one day why he is there the whole day and he told me that it is because his wife is afraid to be alone there. He monitors her eating, pills, exercise, physical therapy, and bed changing. The staff is very diligent with her because they are being watched like a hawk. A great example of a husband loving his wife the way that Christ loved his church! He is sacrificing everything, every day, to protect and help his wife. Love really is patient and kind in the case of this man.

I have to feed my mother's cat twice a day and water her plants. She was very clear on those things. I visited her twice a day at the rehabilitation center. The price of gas was rising and was up to nearly four dollars. It had been a rapid increase since we proclaimed war on terror. It was making travel difficult for us because Guy did not have a salary, but we could still find a thing or two to sell at auction or a garage sale that was keeping gas in the car and food on the table for now.

One afternoon, I walked in and my mother told me about a patient advocate that had visited her and talked with her. She then showed me a CD that the woman had given her to listen to when she goes home. I went to the patient advocate's office and asked her if she had been witnessing to my Mom. Her face went as white as a sheet and with much trepidation she said, "yes?. I said to her, "Please don't stop". The color immediately returned to her face and she smiled with a sigh of relief. She said, "I thought you came in here to reprimand me for sharing my faith". I told her that I was a Christian and that I am appreciative of anyone who will discuss Jesus with my Mom.

In Ukrainian, there is an adage that loosely translated says, "The egg does not teach the chicken". Hence, my mother is more apprehensive about listening to me, the egg, than to listen to others. She does know that Jesus is the Son of God, died and was buried, and then was resurrected from the dead. I am not sure of her salvation because her generation considered it a private matter. Having been raised in a Communist country, she was not allowed to read the bible, but her grandmother would have her read it under the cover of night. Her grandmother had it memorized because she was illiterate and would correct my mother when she tried to skip parts just to finish earlier. In a way, she was able to read God's word without the indoctrination of a church or denomination. I know that God has used that for her good because she was my first bible. My concern was in the not knowing if she had a personal relationship with Christ.

The patient advocate visited her every day and spoke to her about the bible. She told me one day that my mother was fine and for me not to worry. She assured me that God knows my mother's heart and that he is in there. I prayed that God's word would not return void. Then it hit me. We are to ask as if we have received it and it will be given to us. What better prayer than for someone's salvation? We tend to give God our wish lists and hope that we get something off the list or we pray for health and healing, to find a mate, all things that are centered on us. But what if praying unselfishly for what pleases God genuinely, is done? That may be what is meant by desiring God's will...that none shall perish. My epiphany for the day...

Chapter Eleven
New Opportunities

With all of the frustrations of not being able to help financially support our family, I made a decision and approached Guy with it.

"I want to go back to school and finish my degree."

"Okay."

"Okay?"

"Yes, I support you 100%."

On that note, I called Liberty University's Distance Learning Program and requested all the necessary information and paperwork. After a few weeks of getting transcripts and applying for financial aid, I was enrolled for the fall semester. It has been twenty years since I had attended college. Now that all the pieces were in place, I became nervous. Not sure if I could handle the material at this age, I began to second guess my decision. I knew that other than retaining water, my retention was not all that good. I was concerned about juggling home, my mother's condition, and school after being out of practice for so long. I was then reminded, that it is a matter of discipline and tenacity. "Fear not" for fear is the opposite of faith and I needed to have faith to get this done. I was determined to finish what I had started so long ago.

Liberty accepted thirty-eight out of my forty-eight credits from Fairleigh Dickinson University. It was certainly more than I had anticipated. When I had stopped going to college after my second son was born back in 1986, I was concerned that all those credits and expense would be wasted. Now, to have those applicable to my current status was beyond imaginable. Not only did I not waste my parents' money but all the hard work that had gone into my classes was paying off. I now had the privilege of finishing what I had started.

I had previously been an English Major but that was not offered at Liberty's Distance Learning Program. I then took Psychology since that was a secondary interest of mine. I had many credits in Psychology already because I had found the field fascinating and a good background for a young writer to understand the workings of the mind. It's funny how even then God was preparing what would be laid ahead for me two decades later.

My classes started in August and I was filled an excitement that I did not expect. I was hungry to learn and I was anxious to get my degree now that I had made the commitment.

Finances were still a struggle and Guy and I decided that it was time to look for a job. It had been five years since 9/11 and nothing had changed. Although Guy had been diligently working, regular payroll had not been reinstated since before the terrorist attacks. Everyone at the company was suffering and yet, surprisingly only three people had left in the last five years. By now the insurance settlement must have been secured, yet, we saw none of it to compensate for the back pay. But it was time to move on. We prayed that God would open doors that need to be opened and close the doors that should not be opened. We failed to ask for wisdom to see the difference.

Several job opportunities were available. One was in the field that Guy has worked for decades. He applied and was called in for an interview. We prayed over every step of the process. Desperation for stability was at its peak. It was now November of 2006. After the interview, he had to take an online personality test that was quite extensive. After the owner had the opportunity to review the results, she would let him know if he qualified for the position. A few days had passed and she contacted him about the questionnaire. She said that after reviewing it, she did not feel that he was a good fit for the company. Much like Sarah addressing Abraham, I turned to Guy and said that he needs to go in person and try again, "convince her to hire you", I advised him. "We cannot afford to go without another paycheck. He made an appointment to come in for a second chance interview. During the interview, the boss re-evaluated his qualifications, years of experience, and his previous programming abilities. She decided to hire him. She established that it would be a good idea for him to read a few books and handed him the books. He took them and held them in his arms which apparently caused her to take them from him and reposition them to be "properly" held. I really hoped that this was not a sign of things to come.

The arrangement was that he would have a salary for the first two months. After that time, he would receive a draw against commissions. Fair enough. The market was still a bit tough and he was now entering into new ground in a new state. All of his old New York contacts had dried up and were gone. He would in essence, be starting all over again. Cold calling is considered a beginner's arena but when you are in a new area, you have to use all tools at hand, even the more primitive ones. Guy is not afraid to work hard and starting from scratch still means a paycheck so, cold calling it is.

As time went on, it became apparent that his boss needed to control every detail. The tip off was in the way she corrected him for carrying the books but c'est la viev. Hindsight and only hindsight is twenty-twenty. He virtually had to stop every fifteen minutes to log in the events for the previous fifteen minutes. If you know anything about sales, it breaks the momentum of doing cold calling. But Guy persevered. He started networking in the area and meeting other businesses. He did what he does best: work hard, get his name out there, and take good care of his clients.

Six months had passed and the tension in the office was immeasurable. There was a lot of turnover in the small company over several months. Employees were resisting the overbearing personality of the boss and some made a choice to leave as a result of it. One or two people said that they did not receive their last check once they gave notice.

Guy had been contemplating leaving but wanted to make sure he had another job lined up first. During one of the networking events, he had met a CEO of a small business that provided telecomm services. He came to like this person and discussed opportunities. The CEO offered him a job. It was the right time and the right type of company for Guy. Even its location was in a city which is where Guy feels at home. He accepted the offer. Now the concern was how to break it to his current boss.

We are strong believers in doing the right thing, following protocol, giving two weeks' notice, but in realizing that there was a potential not to receive his last paycheck, the paycheck fell on the time when our mortgage is due, was very risky for us. He decided for the first time in his life, not to give the two weeks' notice. Instead, on Thursday, he approached his boss, told her that it would be his last day because he was starting with the other company on Monday. He offered to continue to follow up with the clients that were close to closing a deal and then switch them over to her. He wanted this; process to be as painless as possible. She did not talk to him for the rest of the day except to tell him that she insists that he show up on Friday for the whole day.

On Friday, he came into the office and was told to immediately surrender all of his files, all of his contact lists, and databases while being supervised. Then he needed to finish out the day. He had nothing to do but to call his clients to let them know that the owner would now be taking over his leads and introduce her name to them. He finished the calls informing them that she will be getting in touch with them shortly. At the end of the business day, Guy breathed a sigh of relief to go home and went to say goodbye to his boss. As he approached her office, she handed him a letter. The letter stated that he was required to give two weeks' notice and that she is losing money with his abrupt departure. She had paid for special training for him that she wants reimbursed and she is demanding that he pay back his draw for the last four months since the commissions had never finalized. Guy was flabbergasted. She added that there is no way that his clients would be willing to talk to her, so all that time and effort was a waste. Guy tried to explain that he had already spoken to them and that they were all expecting her call. He would still work with her to close the deals and not even ask for the commissions just to make things easy on her. He gave her the list of clients in the pipeline and left.

When Guy came home he told me the news. I was upset but the more I thought about it, the more it didn't make sense. I assumed the letter was an emotional retaliation for leaving without notice. I believed that she would calm down after a few days and this would all be behind us. It was a small company and I think she just took it very personally. I tried to put it out of my mind and just enjoy the weekend.

A few weeks had passed and we never heard from Guy's former boss again. He was enjoying his new job and was very excited about it. He felt like himself again and it was refreshing to see him so energetic and motivated. Perhaps healing was upon us. One evening, Guy must have been working late or stuck in traffic because he did not come home at his usual time. I was home alone when someone in a cowboy hat rang our doorbell. It was not an unusual sight because people always stop by to purchase chickens, goats, eggs, or vegetables. The strange thing was, that he rang the bell and then started to walk around the outside of the house. I was home alone and it was already dark outside. I felt frightened. I did what anyone would do in a b rated movie, I grabbed a flashlight and went outside. I don't know what I was thinking. Just as I turned the corner, this man creeped around the side and startled me. I gave a yell and I think my feet actually left the ground. He said he was sorry that he scared me, he was just trying to go to the other door. I quickly noticed that he had an official look and was carrying a gun. I asked, "How can I help you?" He then asked if I'm Guy's wife. My heart dropped to my stomach. I could not hear what he said after that because of the pounding of my heart was so loud. I was afraid that the news would be really bad, that Guy was not coming home to me anymore. With great trepidation I replied, "yes?. He handed me an envelope, I assumed it was his personal affects and he then asked me to sign on his clipboard. After I did, he told me that we had just been served. Relief washed over me that he was not here to inform me that my husband was lying in a ditch somewhere. Simultaneously, a new flood of fear came over me, what does this mean? We had never been sued before and this was so formal that I did not know what to expect. I waited anxiously for Guy to get home and get comfortable. After he had settled in, I told him about the lawsuit. We discussed it for a while and we both felt very uneasy about the whole thing but the reality was, we were being sued and we needed to come up with a game plan. We put it to rest for the evening and decided to address it over the next few days. After a couple of days, Guy and I both came to the conclusion of not getting upset and what will be will be. It helps at times to take the worst case scenario and come to terms with it because anything less is automatically acceptable. We put it in God's hands and drew on the trust that whether we win or lose, God is allowing this for our good.

For a while now, we have been speaking with our local senator's office in regard to regaining Guy's lost wages. The senator had set us up with the chancellor of the labor boards and pushed our case through faster. We had a date to appear for arbitration and we would be seeing his 9/11 boss for the first time since Guy left the company. We spent the time gathering up all the documents we had including emails and income tax returns to show that his salary had suddenly declined after 9/11. The emails showed that his boss promised to pay his wages and back pay. It was an open and shut case.

The day arrived and we travelled to Trenton, NJ for the arbitration. Outside of the building, Guy's boss confronted us. He said that he understands Guy's need to take him through these channels and wants us to know that there are no hard feelings. He understands that he owes us money and that no matter what happens today, he is still very fond of Guy, and will take care of him. This is just a formality but we had his assurance that he will do the right thing. A warm feeling filled me towards his boss. They had all been through so much but especially Guy and his two co-workers who were actually there on 9/11. Everyone has had their own part to endure and we knew it had not been easy for his boss to stay afloat. Under better circumstances, he was really a nice employer. But character is not determined by how you conduct yourself during good times but rather about how you conduct yourself during hard times.

We all went upstairs and met before the chancellor of the NJ Labor Boards. We could not afford an attorney for this but his boss did have an attorney. It did not seem to be necessary. Some say that when one hires an attorney it can be construed as a sense of guilt therefore needing legal representation. I do not know how accurate that is. I do know that it is prudent to have an attorney but recognize that the attorney's job is merely filing the necessary paperwork and translating what you tell him or her into legaleze; at least that has been my personal experience. You need to know your rights and how to plead your case and then let the attorney use the legal jargon to do so.

Once the discussion commenced, the chancellor asked a few preliminary questions. One of them was addressed to Guy's former boss and the question was, "Was Guy Yasika in your employment". The answer that came from his boss astonished us, "Not after 9/11. The company had dissolved after the terrorists attacks." The chancellor seemed taken aback by this response and asked, "But wasn't Guy reporting to work along with other employees every day?. The reply came, "No, they were just gathering together at the New Jersey office to support one another during this time." The chancellor asked if this was just for a few hours or all day and the response was all day. At this point, the chancellor said that when people "gather" at an office every day, all day, we call that showing up for work.

Many more statements were made that left us thunderstruck. In the middle of the arbitration, the ex-boss was getting very heated. His speech became aggressive, his volume was escalated, his breathing was more rapid. He stood up at one point and said that he apologizes but needs to go pick up his kids and proceeded to leave. His lawyer tried to advise him not to and then the chancellor suggested rather kindly, for him to call someone to pick up the children for him since we were not done here. It was surreal. It was so ridiculous that it was funny. I could tell that Guy was starting to boil. Our open and shut case was turning into a sideshow. He and I talked a little just to be able to laugh and release some stress. The opposition's lawyer came over to us and said that our relationship is admirable. He could tell that we had something unusual and that we shared a special bond. He had that with his wife as well which is why he was able to recognize it. We thanked him sincerely and said please don't think that we were laughing at anyone or anything. We were laughing to relieve the stress. He told us that he already knew that and said it was nice to see a couple like us. We thanked him again and he returned to his side of the room.

The ex-boss was able to find someone to pick up his kids so he sat down and the procedure continued. The company that Guy had worked for had changed names twice after 9/11. Our claim was for each of the companies. While we would never see the four and a half years of salary that he owed us, we were hoping to at least recuperate some of it. At the time we filed with the labor boards, the cap on recovering funds was $10,000. Afterwards they had increased the cap to $30,000. So our first claim was for $10,000 followed by two more claims of $30,000. If we were to win, the award is $70,000. Many people would find that to be a considerable settlement. But we are not talking about a lawsuit settlement. This is about receiving one's salary for working consistently. In that vein, $70,000 divided by four and a half years is not much of a salary. As a matter of fact, it puts us below the poverty level.

The former boss stated that after 9/11 Guy was no longer an employee because he had to downsize the company. We produced paychecks and health insurance statements. His response to these was to say that he did that as a personal favor to give us money once in a while and provide health insurance for us because we were his friends. It had nothing to do with paying him as an employee. Guy then asked in an exasperated voice, "Why then did you send me a W2 at the end of the year and where is the termination letter?" The owner retorted with, "I made a mistake. I didn't care if I got in trouble for helping you. That's what I do." After much heated discussion and, raw emotions, the chancellor went back to his chambers to review the evidence. Upon his return he stated that he does not believe that the former employer was trying to help Guy but rather that in every sense of the word, he was an employee up until the date that we had given. He awards us $10,000 for the first company. However, he cannot award us for the other two company names because we have no proof of what the salary conditions were. We had produced the original offer letter, and while the company names had changed, nothing had changed with regard to the employment status. But, the ruling determined that we needed to provide evidence with the new company names stating the salary agreement because for all they know, we could have agreed to this drastic cut in pay. The employer had 45 days to appeal this and if he chose not to, then he would be expected to pay by the 45th day. He could however, pay sooner if he desired.

As it stood, we had lost a ton of money. We were concerned that he would appeal the case or just refuse to pay. A few times in the past we would meet with the ex-boss to get an understanding of what was happening and if we were any closer to getting the back pay. Time and time again, we believed him when he told us that the money was coming. He would seem so sincere and so concerned about our wellbeing that we trusted him. But we did reach a point where we were no longer so convinced. At the last meeting, we went and met for coffee. I had a tape recorder in my purse which I placed on the table. (In the state of New Jersey, it is legal to record a conversation without the knowledge of the other person as long as the person recording is a party to the conversation). We asked the usual questions about when the back pay was coming and when can we expect the regular paychecks to resume. My heart was palpitating at the prospect of being caught with the tape recorder. Thankfully, we left undetected. The recording turned out to be a bit muffled and had picked up a lot of the background sound but the words were still quite distinguishable. Thus, I wanted to present the tape to the chancellor but Guy advised me to wait in case there was an appeal at which time we would be able to unequivocally prove that this money was owed to us. We left very discouraged. As we emerged from the building, my eye caught a glimpse of a woman across the street. Guy was so mad and kept reviewing the points of the arbitration. I listened but my eyes kept drifting over to the woman across the street. She was sitting on a curb of a church and looked like she was crying. I had a need to go over to her but after the emotions of the day, I really was not in the mood to deal with a stranger at this point. Yet, once again, the urging was intense. I asked Guy to come with me but he just could not bring himself to calm down but he told me to go ahead.

I crossed the street and approached the woman. I asked her if she was alright. She looked up, smiled, and she that she was alright. I then asked her if I could pray with her. She happily said yes. We prayed and at the end she grabbed my arm and said, "God bless you". I thanked her and walked away. The thought crossed my mind that maybe all of what we went through to get our money back was designed so that I would meet that woman. Only God knows the purpose but I know that there was a purpose that served God.

The forty-five days were up and there was no appeal. There also was no check. We called the chancellor and asked what the next step would be to reinforce the decision. He told us that we now have to contact the sheriff's department to enforce the order. The first part would involve the sheriff's office going to his house and delivering the decision. Then, they would take inventory of his assets if he did not produce a check. We needed to send a $35.00 processing fee to the sheriff's office and that would get the ball rolling.

Many weeks had passed and we received a response from the sheriff's office. They did go to the house and do inventory but most things were not in the ex-boss's name. A short while after words, we received a legal document from his lawyer informing us that he was filing for bankruptcy. We would never see the money at this point. It was alright. While the principle had been violated, God had still provided our basic needs over the years and that was the most important thing. We were no longer going to focus on the money or on what should have been because that was not rational let alone biblical. We had a grateful heart for all that the Lord had provided.

The lawsuit against us presented a problem of being able to afford legal representation. My brother generously offered to pay for the retainer and wanted to assure Guy that he understands how hard it is to accept help but that this was necessary and that he was glad to do it. We told the lawyer that we could go as far as the retainer and after that, we needed to go pro se. The case involved depositions, avidavits, discovery, and other legal entanglements. When all was said and done, the parties were brought before an arbitrator as a last resort before filing in the court. The arbitrator listened to all the details and decided that there was no specification in the offer letter or contract that stated that Guy would have to repay the draw if commissions were not acquired. The contract should have had specific language stating how much needed to be repaid and the conditions in which they are to be repaid including time frames. Since this was not specified in the offer letter nor in the contract, it is therefore presumed that he was not responsible for repaying the draw. Another point in our favor was that the former boss had forgotten to sign her name on the contract making it null and void. Why this was not determined in the very beginning of the case alludes me but two years later and thousands of dollars invested in the legal system determined Guy's innocence. In approaching this job, we had prayed that doors would be opened that should be opened and that doors that should be closed will be closed, then when Guy did not get it, we kicked the door wide open not respecting the fact that God was closing that door. Another lesson learned. Another chapter was behind us.

Chapter Twelve
Vengence is the Lord's
(and the Navy Seals' too!)

It has been five years since Guy has left the company that was associated with his 911 experience. We are approaching the ten years anniversary. We have a speaking engagement in Indianapolis to commemorate the anniversary and are grateful that people have not forgotten.

In 2009, our oldest son graduated from seminary, and I graduated from my undergrad studies. I have continued with graduate school to get my license for professional counseling. I had been an English major originally and through the events that have happened and the way God has orchestrated my steps, He has led me to share my experiences, wisdom, and understanding with others who are going through difficult times. I am on the counseling team at our church that we offer for free to the community. I did not see any of this in my future but God did. If someone would have told me on September 10th all that would transpire both good and bad, I would not have believed them and I certainly would not have wanted to experience any of it. Now, with hindsight, I am grateful for the trials. I am grateful for all that I have learned and I am grateful for the path that God has laid out for me. I truly count it all joy.

Now in 2011, our youngest son is home with us and our oldest son is getting married this summer. Life continues and we need to know how to live in the world but not be a part of it. People can get through difficulties without knowing God, it happens all the time. The difference is that those who know God do not lament what God has allowed but they have hope and they know that God will work it out for their good. No one can avoid the trials of life but they can learn to change their focus from the winds of the storm to the promises of the Lord.

As I finished up my paper for this semester, I checked my email which provides headlines of the day's news. I could not believe my eyes when I read the headline that Osama Bin Laden was killed. I quickly ran into the bedroom and woke Guy up. I told him softly that I wanted him to hear the news from me. On May 1, 2011, almost exactly ten years later, Bin Laden was killed by the Navy Seals team six! I started crying and I was not sure why. As I thought about it, I realized that we finally had closure to a very long ordeal. It meant something personally to us that the evil reign of Osama Bin Laden was over.

I am not a bible scholar by any means, many will probably argue with some of my biblical statements which is fine, as long as the main thing remains the main thing. It is best not to major on the minors, nor to minor on the majors. The purpose here was to provide our personal testimony of the events of 911 and the aftermath which included God working in our lives every step of the way. Denying the truth does not change the truth. We are eyewitnesses to God's hand in our lives and we are in awe of His love. We were wounded but not broken and in our healing we were restored in a way so miraculous and glorious for we saw a peek into heaven.

THE END

Would you like to see your manuscript become a book?

If you are interested in becoming a PublishAmerica author, please submit your manuscript for possible publication to us at:

acquisitions@publishamerica.com

You may also mail in your manuscript to:

PublishAmerica
PO Box 151
Frederick, MD 21705

www.publishamerica.com

CPSIA information can be obtained at www.ICGtesting.com
Printed in the USA
BVOW072100110712

294995BV00001B/62/P